Introduction

If you have an interest in the game of basketball, then this is the book for you. It is designed for people that want to learn the game and improve their skills. This book will give you the foundation necessary to compete at any level, from rec center pickup games to collegiate basketball. Players of all ages and skill levels can gain a better understanding of basketball from the information provided in this book. By the end, you'll be able to take your game to the next level and compete against the best players around.

What Will You Get Out of This Book?

What you can expect to get out of this book depends on your current skill level and basketball experience. Players with no basketball experience can expect to learn the basics of basketball from simple terminology to advanced offensive and defensive concepts. Players with basketball experience can skip to a section that interests them or head straight to the Drills chapter. All players can learn to improve their game through this book.

What Concepts Will You Learn?

You will learn about player positions, ball-handling, passing, shooting, rebounding, defense, defensive sets, offensive techniques, steals, and blocks. This information is broken up into several chapters in which I discuss each concept in depth. I will also cover several offensive and defensive moves and techniques that you can use in specific situations. You will learn everything you need to know to improve your basketball ability. Learning is the most important aspect of this book. I want you to learn new things and hopefully come to enjoy basketball even more.

How Much Will You Improve?

Your overall improvement will depend on three factors: how good you want to become, your dedication to improve, and the level of competition you want to prepare for. How skilled you actually want to become will be a big factor in your overall improvement. If you want to make it to the professional level, you will have to work much harder than a player that wants to dominate a recreation league. Dedication is also an important factor. You will see the greatest improvement if you are dedicated to getting better. You have to put forth consistent effort to truly improve your skill level. Lastly, the level of competition you're preparing for will make a big difference. For example, you will need to possess a higher skill level to play on a collegiate level as opposed to a high school level. The level of competition increases quite substantially at each level.

What is the Goal of This Book?

The goal of this book is for you to become the best basketball player that you can possibly be. The better you become at the game, the easier it will become. As it gets easier, you will find that the competition isn't as tough as it once was. The more skilled you become at something, the more fun it becomes and basketball is no different. You may even discover that basketball is more fun than it was before. You have the opportunity to reach your full potential and become the best player you can be.

Acknowledgements

I'd like to give a special thanks to the UNT basketball team, their coaches, and their assistant sports information director for allowing me to get all the necessary pictures for this book. I couldn't have finished it without their cooperation and for that I am thankful.

I would also like to thank my mom for her unwavering belief in me. If not for her continuous support, I'm sure I would never have been able to finish this book. I'm glad that I was able to have such a wonderful person as a mother.

Copyright © 2014 by Tarrence Garrison

All rights reserved. No part of this publication may be reproduced, distributed, or transmit-ted in any form or by any means, including photocopying, recording, or other electronic or mechanical methods, without the prior written permission of the publisher, except in the case of brief quotations embodied in critical reviews and certain other noncommercial uses permitted by copyright law.

Disclaimer

The information in this book is meant to supplement, not replace, proper basketball training. Like any sport involving speed, equipment, balance and environ-mental factors, basketball poses some inherent risk. The author advises readers to take full responsibility for their safety and know their limitations. Before practicing the skills described in this book, be sure that your equipment is well maintained, and do not take risks beyond your level of experience, aptitude, training, and comfort level.

Table of Contents

What is Basketball? 7

Player Positions 14

    Point Guard 14

    Shooting Guard 18

    Small Forward 23

    Power Forward 28

    Center 32

Basic Offensive Techniques 37

Shooting 48

Ball-Handling 57

Passing 67

Attacking the Basket 75

Playing in the Post 79

Rebounding 88

Defense 94

Defensive Sets 102

Steals 115

Blocks 118

Drills 120

Terminology 138

Chapter 1 | What is Basketball?

"Some people want it to happen,

some wish it would happen,

others make it happen"

– *Michael Jordan*

Basketball is a game in which two teams attempt to score points by getting a basketball through the goal. Each team must defend their goal while attempting to score in the opposing team's goal. To score, teams must get the ball through the rim by shooting, dunking, or performing a layup. An attempt to put the ball through the goal is called a field goal attempt. Field goals can yield two to three points depending on where they're taken. Successful field goals that are taken inside the three-point line result in two points. Field goals taken outside the three-point line, or three-pointers, result in three points. Successful free throws only result in one point.

To win a basketball game, one team must outscore the opposing team before the game ends. If the score is tied at the end of a game, then that game will go into overtime.

To advance the ball up the court, players must dribble or pass it to teammates. Whenever a player moves with the ball, he or she must dribble it to avoid committing a traveling violation. At its core, basketball is a simple game, but it can be complicated when all the different strategies and styles of play are factored in.

Designated Positions

Basketball includes five different positions: point guard, shooting guard, small forward, power forward, and center. Each player on the court is usually assigned to one of these five positions. Each position has different responsibilities and roles on offense and defense.

Strategy

Strategy is one of the most important elements of basketball. There exist both offensive and defensive plays that teams can use to their advantage. Some offensive plays are more effective against certain defenses and vice versa. Teams must be able to analyze what the opposing team is doing and make adjustments to outplay their opponents. The game of basketball (especially at higher levels of competition) is commonly compared to chess in that both games require strategy.

Different Levels of Competition

Basketball has several different levels of competition that greatly differ in skill and athletic ability. Usually, as the level of competition increases, players will become more physically imposing, skilled, and make use of more advanced basketball techniques. Teams at higher levels will carry out more complicated strategies and the competition will become increasingly fierce. Also, some of the rules are subject to change at the different levels of competition.

Youth Level

The lowest level of competition is the youth level. This level is broken up into different age groups that are usually separated by just a single year. The level is full of kids that are just beginning to play basketball. These kids may not yet fully understand the game or may lack proper fundamental skills. Some of the younger leagues lower the goals to around seven or eight feet to accommodate the kids' heights. The referees in some of these youth leagues may also be lax with the rules to allow the children to have fun. This is a great place to start learning about the game of basketball before reaching some of the higher levels of competition.

Middle School Level

The middle school level is where many schools begin to have organized sports teams. This level can be some players' first organized team. It is important to note that there are only a certain amount of positions at each school, so unfortunately, not everyone will be able to make a team. This level may feature more skilled players than the previous level, but it is not uncommon for players to still lack fundamental skills and basketball knowledge.

High School Level

The high school level is where the competition begins to get more serious. Players at this level begin to grasp the fundamentals and become more skilled at the game of basketball. This level includes both high school and summer leagues teams. There are players at this level who are skilled enough to play professional basketball, though this is rare.

Collegiate Level

The collegiate level features some of the fiercest competition and is the toughest level so far. Players at this level are no longer young teenagers, but adults. Many of these players have a good grasp of the fundamentals and possess advanced basketball skills. The collegiate level is split into divisions that often correspond to the skill level of the players that compete in them. In order of the level of competition (from lowest to highest), the divisions are Division 3, Division 2, and Division 1 basketball programs. The National Collegiate Athletic Association (NCAA) organizes all of these divisions. Division 1 basketball programs feature some of the best players in the country.

International Level

The international level is a professional level of basketball that is played in different countries around the world. There are various leagues that features different skill levels and have a hierarchy similar to that of collegiate basketball. Players at this level, depending on the league, are highly skilled. In is not uncommon for an

American player to finish college and receive a contract to play basketball in another country. Several of the best international leagues are located in Europe.

Professional Level

This is the highest level of basketball and features some of the best players in the world. This level features the National Basketball Association, which is considered to be the very highest level of basketball competition. The NBA has a long history of outstanding basketball players such as Michael Jordan, Magic Johnson, and Bill Russell. The Women's National Basketball Association is essentially the same as the NBA, but reserved only for women.

To make it into the NBA, players must have an extremely high-level of skill and/or athletic abilities. The NBA and WNBA are not the only high-level professional leagues. There is also the National Basketball Development League, Athletic Basketball Association, and International Basketball League.

Equipment

Very little equipment is needed to play a regular game of basketball – a basketball, a flat surface to play on, and two goals facing each other on opposite ends of the surface. However, a competitive basketball game requires a few other items such as scoreboards, score sheets, uniforms, and clocks.

The basketball is ultimately the same size for all levels of play. The exception is that males and females have different sized basketballs. For males, the basketball has a 29.5-inch circumference and weighs 22 ounces. For females, the basketball is 28.5 inches in circumference and weighs 20 ounces. Most basketballs in the United States are black and orange though some countries use a white and orange ball.

Basketball courts vary in length depending on the level of play. For example, international levels have a 91.9 by 49.2 foot court while professional and collegiate courts are 94 by 50 feet. The rim is set 10 feet off the ground in every level of competition with the exception of some youth leagues. It is important that the rim is set to the correct height and in the middle of the backboard or it could affect the game.

Regulation

Regulation times may vary depending on the level of competition and the league. Games are usually divided into quarters. High school, FIBA (or other international leagues), and NBA games are all split up into four quarters of varied lengths. High school games have 8-minute quarters, FIBA features 10-minute quarters, and the NBA uses 12-minute quarters. Each overtime period is five minutes in length except in high school games, which are only four minutes.

Five players from each team are allowed to be on the court at a time. To be eligible to compete, a team must have a least five healthy players on their roster. If a situation occurs that limits a team's number of players to anything less than five, then that team must forfeit the game.

Substitutions allow players on the bench to enter the game. Teams can substitute players as often as they like. Substitutions can even play into the overall strategy of the game if used properly.

Each team gets a set amount of timeouts that they can use to halt play. Timeouts allow coaches to meet with their players to discuss strategies or allow the players to take a quick break to recuperate.

On the sideline, there is usually a head coach, an assistant coach, sports trainers, and reserve players. For the most part, the head coach makes the decisions for the team regarding strategy, substitutions, plays, and timeouts. The assistant coaches make suggestions to the head coach and give strategy advice to players. The trainers are there to take care of any injuries that may occur during the course of a game.

Rules

Basketball has a number of rules in place. Breaking one of these rules will result in a violation and the ball will awarded to the opposing team. Here are a few common violations that everyone should know:

Traveling: A violation that occurs when a player fails to dribble the ball before moving both feet. It also occurs if the player, in possession of the ball, jumps into the air and lands while still in possession of the ball.

Double dribble: A violation that occurs when the ball-handler picks up the ball while dribbling and then resumes dribbling later.

Three-second violation: A violation that occurs when an offensive player stands in the painted area for three seconds.

Carrying: A violation that occurs when the ball-handler allows the ball to come to rest or pauses while dribbling.

Goaltending: A violation that occurs when a player interferes with the ball while it is in contact with the rim. If the offense commits the goaltending violation, the ball will be awarded to the opposing team. If the defense commits the goaltending violation, the offense will be awarded the points for the field goal attempt.

Out-of-bounds: The ball cannot touch the ground outside of the boundary of the court (or the out-of-bounds line). If an offensive player is the last one to make contact with the ball, then it will result in a turnover. The ball is allowed to go over the line as long as it does not touch the ground. This enables players to jump out of bounds to save the basketball and keep it in play.

Fouls

Fouls are the result of illegal physical contact with another player. There are two types of fouls: defensive and offensive. Defensive fouls are the most common type committed during a game. They include reaching, shooting, over-the-back, and blocking fouls. Committing a defensive foul will result in a stoppage of play and the offensive team will retain possession of the basketball. Shooting fouls will automatically result in one to three free throws (depending on where the field goal was attempted and whether or not it was made) for the offensive player who was fouled. Offensive fouls are not as common as defensive fouls, but they still occur with some regularity during a basketball game. The most common type of offensive foul is a charging foul. Offensive fouls result in a turnover and the ball will be awarded to the opposing team. Offensive fouls are harmful for the offensive team because they lead to wasted possessions.

Displaying poor sportsmanship can result in a special type of foul, called a technical foul. This type of foul can be called against players and coaches. A technical foul can be the result of (among other things) cursing and/or fighting. Repeated technical fouls will result in an ejection (of the player who committed the fouls) from the game. If a technical foul is called, the other team will be awarded free throws. The team may choose any of their players on the court to shoot the free throws. The rules associated with this situation vary from league to league.

Another special type of foul is an intentional foul, which results from intentional, excessive physical contact with another player. Players who commit intentional fouls may also be ejected from the game.

Each team has a limited number of fouls they are allowed to commit within a certain amount of time. Exceeding this limit will place the team "in the penalty." When a team is in the penalty the opposing team will be awarded free throws for both shooting and non-shooting fouls. For non-shooting fouls, the opposing team will be awarded only one free throw. However, if the first free throw is made, the shooter will be awarded a second free throw. This situation is called a one-and-one. In high school and college, a team will be awarded a one-and-one if the opposing team reaches seven fouls during a half and two free throws if ten or more fouls are made. The number of fouls varies for professional and international leagues. The penalty is reached in four fouls for the NBA and FIBA leagues.

The referee can decide whether to call a foul or not. Referees often use discretion and their best judgment when calling fouls. As in any sport, there are times when the referees don't make a call or make an incorrect call.

Photo by Rick Yeatts

Chapter 2 | Player Positions

"My greatest gift that I have in life is basketball."
– Isiah Thomas

Point Guard

The point guard position is one of the most important and flexible positions in the game of basketball. This position usually starts the offense and distributes the ball to teammates.

The main responsibilities of the position are to facilitate the offense, lead the team on the court, and be an extension of the head coach. Point guards typically bring the ball down the court and call plays for the team to run. They have the option of choosing their own plays to run or running the plays that the head coach selects. On some teams, other positions are allowed to start the offense as well. However, the point guard position initializes the majority of the offensive and defensive plays for a team.

Point guards are expected to be leaders on the court. They are often considered to be extensions of the coach while they are in the game. It is not uncommon for the point guard to be referred to as the "floor general" or the "coach on the court." Many point guards have a close relationship with their coaches because they must work closely with them when issuing instructions to the team.

Key Skills for Point Guards

Being effective at this position requires several skills. Point guards need to be able to handle the ball, pass, and lead their team on the court. These players have the basketball in their hands for the majority of the game so it is imperative that they are able to handle the ball well. They must be able to bring the ball up the court against a defense, which may include breaking through a press. They must also be able to handle the ball while being pressured in a half-court offense. The opposing point guard may be an effective defender; so ball-handling skills at this position are critical. Point guards just need to be comfortable with the basketball so they can get the ball from point A to point B without turning it over.

Point guards need to be able pass the ball and distribute it to teammates. Again, point guards have possession of the basketball for most of the game. They will often have more opportunities to pass the ball than some of the other players on the team. If you were to look at a stat sheet for any basketball game, it is likely that the point guard will have the most assists for a team. Making assists is basically expected of the players at this position. A good point guard should be able to make crisp, accurate passes to teammates in several different situations, especially while being pressured.

The ability to lead is also an important skill for point guards. Coaches often thrust these players into a leadership role by making them the captain of the team. Every point guard should develop some type of leadership ability so they can lead their team through hardships. Players will never know when they'll need to step up and be a leader.

Point guards should also have the ability to score the basketball when the need or opportunity arises. A typical point guard's scoring repertoire may include shooting three-pointers, mid-range shots, or driving and scoring in the paint. All of these methods are viable options for the point position and each should be developed to a certain extent. These skills will allow players to balance out their offensive abilities. For example, point guards that are able to shoot the three may get open opportunities when they are setting up the offense. So if you're a point guard, be sure to develop the offensive abilities that enable you to score in various situations.

Additional Abilities

To a lesser extent, depending on the team, point guards need to possess a few other skills to be successful. They'll need defensive toughness, court awareness, and court vision. Being tough defensively simply refers to how hard the individual player plays on defense. Examples of defensive toughness would include guarding the offensive players closely, containing them, and making it difficult for them to maneuver and make plays. Court vision and court awareness refer to the player's ability to see and understand what's going on around him/her. They allow players to find open teammates on the court. Some point guards possess such high court vision and awareness that they only need to glance at other players to know where they are. They can simply pass the ball to the location where they know their teammates will be. I would argue that these skills are not as important as the ones mentioned earlier, but I believe they are still important skills for a point guard to develop.

Styles of Play

There are several ways that the point guard position can be played. These players have the flexibility score, pass, facilitate the offense, or be defensive stoppers. These various styles of play are what make the position so flexible, though every position could technically be considered flexible.

Passer

The most common style of play for the position is the pass-first point guard. In this style, the point guard looks to pass the ball to teammates rather than actively attempting to score. This play style usually results in the accumulation of assists since the point guard is constantly passing the ball to teammates. The pass-first point guard is not concerned, or should not be concerned, with the amount of points that he/she scores.

Scorer

Score-first point guards look to score the ball as a first option rather than passing it to teammates. This does not necessarily mean that they will not pass the ball to teammates, just that they are looking to take their shot first. This play style is usually for reserved for the point guards that are the star players/scorers of their team. The majority of the time, they will be the team's first option for scoring. This is an attractive play style for many players because it allows them to score the ball, which is the most exciting aspect of basketball for many players. However, many point guards are evaluated by their ability to contribute with their leadership or passing ability, and not by their scoring.

Facilitator

The next play style is the facilitator. Facilitators start the offense and make good basketball decisions. They go with the flow of the offense and contribute when needed, but are not necessarily looking to make big plays. This play style is usually for players that are not skilled at scoring or making plays, but they can be invaluable if they can recognize situations and act accordingly.

Defender

Defensive-minded point guards love to play defense so that they can pester their opponents and force turnovers and/or bad shots. Every point guard should have the defensive ability to contain their opponent, but these defensive specialists really pressure their opponents. This style of play is really impressive to coaches because requires a lot of effort and many coaches focus on the defensive aspect of basketball.

Combination

Players can also combine these play styles together. They can look to score and pass to teammates, facilitate the offense and be defensive-minded, or offer a little bit of each. Players at the point guard position should evaluate their own strengths and weaknesses before adopting a certain style of play.

The Point Guard Position in a Nutshell

The main role of the point guard position is to start the offense and pass the ball to the right teammate at the right time. Most great point guards are evaluated by their ability to make the smart play. Think of all the great point guards from the past and present. Most of them got the ball where it needed to be and made the right plays to benefit their team. They were unselfish and tried as hard as they could to help their team win. So if you are trying to develop the skills to be a great point guard, you should start by trying to get the ball where it needs to be for your team to be successful.

Shooting Guard

The shooting guard position is usually reserved for a team's best shooters. These shooters are often the go-to players for shooting the basketball, whether it's for three-pointers, mid-range, or pull-up jumpers off the dribble. The position is very versatile in what the player is allowed to do on offense, which makes it one of the most exciting positions in basketball. This position is widely considered to be a scoring position and is also commonly referred to as the two-position.

The main responsibilities of this position are to take advantage of open shot opportunities, utilize screens to create open shot opportunities, assist the point guard in bringing the ball up the court, and defend opposing players on defense. Shooting guards are often the go-to players for shooting the basketball. Coaches usually place their best shooters at this position and run plays in an attempt to get them open shot opportunities.

Shooting guards must recognize when they are open and be ready to shoot the ball when the opportunity arises. Recognizing an open shot opportunity, receiving the ball, and taking the shot can all be split-second decisions, so it is important that they stay ready.

These players must also be able to create their own shots by putting the ball on the floor to maneuver past defenders. Shooting guards who are not able to create their own shots will be limited in what they are able to do, so it is important to develop that skill.

Shooting guards should be able to utilize screens to create open shot opportunities as well. They must be able to read the defense and use the screens effectively. For example, if a defender is cheating up on a screen, then the shooting guard can flare out for a shot opportunity. It all depends on how the defender attempts to get around the screen and how effectively the player can read and react. Offensive plays will typically involve the use of screens to get the shooting guard open. In these situations, it is important for the shooting guard to run the defender into the screen. That way, he/she can actually get the opportunity for an open shot attempt.

Shooting guards are able to assist the point guard in bringing the ball up the court or breaking a defensive press. On many teams, the shooting guard is allowed to handle the ball much more than other positions (depending on the situation). This can help relieve some of the pressure from the point guard position. If the point guard is being heavily pressured, then the shooting guard can provide some assistance.

One of the most important responsibilities of the shooting guard position is to defend the opposing team's shooting guards. It is important because the shooting guard position is often the best scorer on a team. Many of the greatest scorers of all-time were shooting guards, such as Michael Jordan. Players of this position must be able to defend the opposing players to contain their scoring output. This means getting through screens, containing, closing out, and keeping track of the opposing player throughout the game. However, depending on the certain factors, such as defensive prowess and the opposing player's skill level, the coach may change the defensive assignments. For example, the shooting guard may defend the small forward position or the point guard may defend the shooting guard position. It is also common for players to switch match-ups during screens.

Key Skills for Shooting Guards

Shooting guards need certain critical skills to be successful during a game of basketball, though some may be considered more important than others. The skills include shooting, ball-handling, and defensive ability.

Shooting guards are not named for their tendency to not shoot the ball. They need to be able to make open shots with some kind of consistency. Shooting guards should be able to make shots while they are under pressure or when they have a small window of opportunity. They also need to understand how long they have to get their shots off based on how far away a defender is from their position. This means that they know when to take their time as opposed to shooting a quick shot. Shooting guards do not need to be the best shooters on the team, but they need to have, at the minimum, an above average ability to shoot the ball. These players have the option to score in other ways, but many teams design plays that allow them to simply catch and shoot the ball.

Shooting guards should also possess a considerable amount of shooting range, preferably up to the three-point line. Impressive shooting range forces the defense to actively defend these players as opposed to just defending the drive. Shooting range keeps the defender playing up close and keeps the floor spaced out. This makes it difficult for the defender to help out his/her teammates on defense. It also gives the shooting guard's teammates room to maneuver and run the plays effectively. The more range the player possesses, the more effective they'll be on offense. The defense will be unable to use the dreaded 2-3 zone, which can paralyze a team offensively.

Shooting guards need to have the ability to handle the ball so that they can create their own shots off the dribble and bring the ball up the court. Ball-Handling skills will serve any player well, but they are especially important for the point guard and shooting guard positions. If the shooting guard is being pressured or trapped by a defender, then he/she may be able to dribble out of the situation. Ball-Handling ability is especially important for breaking defensive presses and getting past tough defenses.

The last crucial skill for the two-guard position is defensive ability. As discussed earlier, a player at this position is often the top scorer on a team. That's why it is so important that these players are able to contain the opposing shooting guards. If the shooting guard's defensive ability is lacking, then he/she may be a liability to the team's success. At the very least, shooting guards should be able to close out and get through screens on defense. This will help limit the number of open shots the opposing shooting guard will receive.

Additional Abilities

There are other abilities that can improve a shooting guard's overall ability and effectiveness on offense and defense. These abilities include speed, quickness, strength, agility, and jumping ability. These abilities can be useful for every position, and this one is no exception.

Speed will allow players to run the fast break effectively by beating other players down the court. It will also allow players to get the ball up the court quickly so the offense can be initialized. Quickness is useful for getting through screens, beating defenders off the dribble, or creating a shot opportunity.

Strength is useful at this position for several reasons. First, it can be used to defend an opposing player, especially if that player is bigger than the shooting guard. Second, it can be used to power through defenders when driving to the basket or finishing at the rim. Third, it can be used to post up and get good inside position to use post moves. Lastly, it is useful for boxing out and getting good position to rebound the basketball. Strength can add all new dimensions to a shooting guard's game. Many professional shooting guards possess great strength and use it effectively on offense and defense.

Agility and jumping ability are two of the most useful and sought after abilities in basketball. These two abilities will help on defense, when driving to the goal, and when finishing at the rim.

All of these abilities can be considered important (depending on whom you ask) for the shooting guard position. Any player at this position should try to add each of them to their repertoire.

Styles of Play

There are several ways that the shooting guard position can be played. The style of play that is chosen depends on the skill of the player and the needs of the team. The styles of play include scorer, passer, and defensive.

Scorer

With the scorer play style, there are a few different ways that shooting guards can score the ball. They can be slashers, three-point, mid-range, or pull-up shooters. Slashers are the players that drive to the basket. They take defenders off the dribble and finish at the rim (or draw a foul). This style of play is very effective against man-to-man defenses or when the floor is spaced out on offense. This is also where ball-handling skills and quickness come into play for the position. The slasher style of play is a common option for many shooting guards, professional or otherwise.

The three-point shooter is also a common style of play for many shooting guards. These players are accurate from behind the three-point line and shoot the majority of their shots from this range. Many offensive plays are designed to get the shooting guard open to take three-point shots. This style of play is difficult for the defense because it forces them to run a man-to-main defense instead of a zone. This spreads out the floor and allows the offense to flow more efficiently.

The mid-range shooter scoring style is for the players that possess a 15 to 20 foot shooting range. Mid-range shooters usually catch the ball and shoot it from this distance by moving to an area to get open or by using a screen. This scoring style is easier for the defense to guard than the previous one. These players possess fairly good range on their jump shot, which extends to just inside of the three-point line. Depending on what type defense is being used, the offensive player may have to create his/her own shot. This can be accomplished by continuously moving through screens or by using an offensive move. Players using this style should test their shot in a variety of scenarios.

The pull-up shooter can be synonymous with the mid-range shooter. I only added this extra play style because it can differ depending on how a player uses it. Pull-up shooters can dribble down the court, stop, and shoot the ball in a fluid motion without being off-balance. They can also shoot in transition or when coming directly off a screen. This scoring style is usually combined with others to add some variety to a player's shot repertoire.

Passer

The next style is the passing shooting guard. In this style, the shooting guard will look to pass the ball first instead of trying to get an open shot. This style of play can be used if a shooting guard lacks the ability to shoot, but is able to pass the ball well. Alternatively, it can be used if the coach wants two shooting guards on the court at the same time. This style of play is not very common, but it is still used by some players.

Defensive

The last style of play is the defensive-minded shooting guard. This style of play is focused on getting defensive stops and containing the opposing shooting guard. Coaches love this type of player because they usually put forth a lot of effort to stop opposing players on defense. These players may or may not be good scorers, but they make up for it by being tenacious defenders. Players that choose this play style should try to develop a consistent jump shot to go along with it. This will make them a threat on offense and defense.

Whichever style of play you choose be sure to try your best to develop a well-rounded game. You will become an asset for your team and a serious threat for the opposing team.

The Shooting Guard Position in a Nutshell

The main role of the shooting guard is to score the basketball by shooting when they're open, driving to the basket, and/or creating their own shot off the dribble. The position is usually reserved for the team's best scorers, but this isn't always the case. There are several ways that the position can be played, and it can occasionally be interchangeable with the point guard position. Players at this position must also be good defenders and have some type of ball-handling ability.

Small Forward

The small forward position is one of, if not the most, flexible positions in the game of basketball. It's a position that is in between the guard and forward positions. It is usually reserved for bigger players who have guard-like skills, but the size of a forward. The small forward position is also known as the three-position.

The main responsibilities of the small forward position are usually scoring, rebounding, and defending. Small forwards can assist the shooting guard in scoring the ball on the perimeter. Unlike the shooting guard position, the small forward position is not really expected to be a great shooter. The way the player chooses to score depends on the individual skill level of that player. There is not a set way that the position is supposed to score. In fact, the small forward position doesn't have to be a scorer at all. They can focus on other aspects of basketball such as rebounding or defense.

The small forward position is expected to rebound the ball. They need to get in the paint and help the post players rebound, even if all they can do is box out. Sometimes an undersized player may fill the position, and it may be difficult for that player to secure the rebound. In this case, it becomes even more crucial that the player boxes out on every defensive possession.

The last responsibility is to defend. This is something that is expected of every player on the team, but like the shooting guard position, many great scorers are small forwards. This makes it very important for the players at this position to be solid defenders. They must be able to stop the opposing small forwards from scoring the basketball. It's also not uncommon for the small forward position to be the best scorer on the team because of the way the position can be played. So it is important that this position is contained on defense.

Small forwards must also be flexible in their defensive abilities. They must be able to quickly close out on shooters, move their feet to cut off a drive, and be strong enough to stop players in the post. The opposing small forward may have the ability to do any, or all, of those things offensively. Many times, small forwards will have the most difficult match-up on defense, so it is crucial for them to build up their defensive capabilities. There are even some small forwards who are not good at anything but defense. These players are defensive specialists that usually take on the toughest defensive assignment in the game. I will discuss this style of play in more detail later.

Key Skills for Small Forwards

Small forwards can choose their skill set based on their size, abilities, skill level, and the needs of the team. Since the position is offensively flexible, it is usually up to the individual player to decide what skills he/she would like to develop. However, I believe that there are a few key skills that every small forward should have. I touched on a few of these previously, but now I will discuss them in more detail.

First, small forwards don't have to be strong offensive players, but they need to have some way to score the basketball. This will prevent the defense from ignoring them on offense and force defenders to stay with them. It will also spread the court and allow the offense to run smoothly. Small forwards can be great shooters, slashers, post players, or a combination of each. I will elaborate more on this later, but for now just think of the position as offensively flexible. Players that are able to score at this position will become a valuable asset for any team.

The next key skill to develop is rebounding. Rebounding is very important at this position because it relieves some of the pressure from the post players. Small forwards must be able to box out on offense and defense when a shot is attempted. They should be able to at least keep the opposing player from getting the ball. The development of this skill is crucial to a team's success because rebounding is such an important factor in a game.

Defense is the last important skill that needs to be developed. It is also widely considered to be the most important skill for this position. Small forwards will need quickness, lateral quickness, and strength. Quickness will help players get through screens and defend other guard positions. Lateral quickness will help prevent a drive to the goal. Lastly, strength will help players defend bigger opponents and rebound more effectively. Strength will not only be beneficial for defense, but for offense as well.

Those are the three crucial skills that should be developed by every player at the small forward position. Small forwards don't have to be great at any one of them, but they should make an effort to develop them all to a respectable level.

Additional Abilities

There are other skills that can make small forwards even more of a threat on offense and defense. These skills can make them better defenders and offensive threats. The skills include athleticism, ball-handling, and passing ability.

Athleticism will benefit the player on both offense and defense. On offense, athleticism may include jumping ability, agility, and speed. Jumping ability can assist the player in blocking shots on defense. It's difficult to get off a layup or a shot when the defender can out-jump you. On offense, jumping ability can add a new dimension to the player's game. It can allow him/her to get higher off the ground on a jump shot, out-jump the defense on layups, or dunk the ball. Achieving this ability can be very beneficial to a player's overall game. Agility can allow players to quickly change directions when handling the ball or defending opponents. Agility is actually a combination of physical abilities, all of which are related to basketball. Speed can be used to outrun the opposing players during fast breaks or while getting back on defense. Possessing all of these athletic abilities will definitely make a player, at the small forward position, more of a threat on the court.

Ball-handling at this position can be used to bring the ball up the court, drive to the basket, or simply handle the ball on the perimeter. Small forwards, like point and shooting guards, can bring the ball up the court if necessary, which can be helpful against tough full-court defenses. They can also use their ball-handling skills to get to the goal against tough defenders. Lastly, they can dribble around the perimeter to get to a certain spot or make use of ball screens. This is a very important skill for players to possess, especially at this position.

The last skill is passing ability. Passing ability is important at this position because it allows players to make assists and get the ball where it needs to be on offense. This will help limit turnovers from bad passes and allow the offense to run smoothly.

All of these skills can be combined to create a very well rounded, skilled small forward. Players at this position should attempt to develop all of them to a certain extent and take their game to the next level.

Styles of Play

Small forwards can choose from several different styles of play, each having their own advantages and disadvantages. The styles include scorers (either guard or post oriented), rebounders, defenders, or a combination of each.

Scorer

There are a few different scoring styles that small forwards can adopt. First, the player can be a shooter. Like the shooting guard position, small forwards are often able to shoot the ball from various ranges. They can be three-point, mid-range, pull-up, or short-range shooters. It all depends on the player's skill level. Small forwards that can shoot the three can be very helpful to their team. These players give the offense another option in the event that a three-pointer needs to be taken. Mid-range and pull-up shooters can also be very effective at this position, especially if they are able to create their own shots. Coaches will often run plays to get the small forward open to take a 15 to 20 foot shot. This scoring style is very common, as there are many players at this position who can consistently make shots.

Small forwards can also be slashers and adept at driving to the basket. Ball-handling skills are important for this style. If the player doesn't have good ball-handling skills, then it will be easier for defenders to steal the ball. The slasher play style is also common at this position, as many professional players are good at driving to the basket. Often, players will be fouled while driving to the basket or finishing at the rim. This can result in easy points from free throws and benefit the team on offense.

The last scoring style is the small forward post player. These players have the offensive skill set of a post player and can use a variety of post moves to score. Depending on their size, these players can create a mismatch for the defense. They can also take some of the scoring pressure off the power forward and center positions by scoring in the post. This scoring style is not as common as some of the other styles, but it can be very effective (especially if the small forward has guard skills as well). Technically, you don't have to be tall or strong to be effective in the post at this position, but it will be helpful if you are.

Rebounder

The next style of play is the rebounder. This player is focused on getting the rebound on both offense and defense. This style of play is mostly used in conjunction with other play styles or as an extension of the player's skill set. It is one of the more crucial skills for the position, but some small forwards are still not strong rebounders. However, there are several players, at this position, that are tenacious rebounders and usually collect a large number of rebounds during a game.

Defender

The next play style focuses on defense. These players are defensive-minded and make it their duty to stop the offensive players from scoring the ball. A lot of players fit this description. They may not be strong offensive players, but they make up for it on the defensive end of the floor. They are able to pressure the opposing players and cause turnovers to benefit their team.

Small forwards can sometimes be separated into three playing styles. These are the guard type, the post type, or the combination of both. Small forwards usually play their position strictly like a guard or as a combination of both. It is quite rare to find a player who strictly utilizes a post game at this position, but it is not unheard of.

Small Forward Position in a Nutshell

The main role of the small forward is basically up to that player and the coach. The player's skill level and the needs of the team will usually dictate what role they will take on during a game. This role may be subject to change based on what the opposing team does or if the player's assignment changes. Basically, small forwards will use whatever skills they currently possess during a game. If they are good shooters, then that may be their role; if they are strictly defensive stoppers, then their role may be to stop the best scorer on the opposing team. I personally believe that the most important role for this position is to defend. Small forwards must be able to stop the opposing players from scoring the ball. So, the main role for the small forward position is to defend and the secondary role is whatever the player is good at.

Power Forward

The power forward position is another flexible position that can be played a few different ways. Power forwards are considered to be post players, but many of them are also able to play on the perimeter, handle the ball, and shoot from long-range. The position's flexibility is similar to that of the small forward position. What players are able to do at this position relies heavily on their skill set and the needs of the team.

The main responsibilities of the position are defending, rebounding, and (occasionally) scoring the basketball. Power forwards must contain their defensive assignments and prevent them from scoring. They must box out on each possession and collect rebounds throughout the game, especially on defense. They must also be able to catch the ball and finish strong in the paint. I will discuss these responsibilities in more detail later in this section.

Key Skills for Power Forwards

Power forwards can possess a number of offensive and defensive skills that will make them invaluable for their team. Of all of these skills, there are a few that are a bit more important than the others. These skills/abilities include: scoring, rebounding, and defending.

Power forwards should have the ability to score the ball in a variety of ways. First, power forwards need to be able to score in the paint. They must be able to catch the ball around the goal and finish with a layup, dunk, or short-range shot. Defenders will attempt to stop them, but they must still be able to score the ball or draw a foul. Second, they must be able to make use of (at least) a few post moves when they catch the ball in the post. Power forwards don't need to have a lot of moves, but they should have a few that they can use when they need to. Lastly, they should be able to consistently make a 10 to 15-foot jump shot. In many offensive sets, the power forward may be positioned on the free throw line or at the short corner. Being able to make shots from these locations will greatly improve their offensive effectiveness.

Rebounding is another important skill that these players need to possess. Since this is a post position, power forwards are expected to be strong rebounders. They must box out opposing players and try to grab as many rebounds as possible. Rebounding at this position also takes some of the rebounding pressure off the center position. The center and power forward positions need to crash the boards together for their team to be successful. There are many drills that can be performed to improve a player's rebounding ability (some of which are listed in the Drills chapter).

The last key skill is defensive ability. At the power forward position, defense can get a little tricky. Not only do they have to defend opposing players in the post, but often have to defend players on the perimeter as well. This is mainly because many players at this position are offensive threats outside of the paint. Power forwards must have the lateral quickness to defend on the perimeter and the strength to keep players out of the paint. In addition to this, they must also be able to contest any shots that are taken in the lane. All of these defensive abilities can be developed with hard work in practice and by gaining experience while playing.

Additional Abilities

There are a few more skills that power forwards can possess. These skills aren't as important as the others but they can add to a player's overall skill level. These skills include ball-handling ability and athleticism (which includes strength and agility).

Ball-handling is a skill that is not required at this position, but it can become a great offensive asset. It allows players to put the ball on the floor to avoid traps and defensive pressure. It can even allow them to create their own shot opportunities by using ball-handling moves or by attacking the goal. It can also allow players to assist in bringing the ball up the court against a defensive press. The Drills chapter has a few drills for improving ball-handling ability.

The next ability is athleticism, which (for this position) consists of strength and quickness. These two abilities are beneficial on both offense and defense. Strength is useful for defending players in the post, boxing out, getting good position, and scoring against defensive resistance. Quickness is useful for containing opposing players, contesting shot attempts, and beating defenders off the dribble. Both of these abilities can be developed with weight and agility training.

Both of these abilities will help make players more well-rounded and effective at this position.

Styles of Play

Like all positions, there are a few different ways that this position can be played. Some power forwards are scorers, rebounders, defenders, or even a combination of all three. The play styles available for this position are closely related to the small forward position and feature some of the same descriptions.

Scorer

The scorer style of play can be split up into three categories (which can be combined): shooter, post player, and slasher. The shooter is the player that mostly uses jump shots to score. Their shooting range usually extends to around 15 feet, but it can go all the way to the three-point line. Shooters are a common style of play for this position and often are combined with other styles of scoring. Depending on the shooter's height and the quickness, they can be very difficult to defend.

The next scorer style is one that uses post moves to score. Since power forwards spend most of their time in the post, it is only natural for them to use post moves to score. Not all power forwards use post moves to score, but those that do can be excellent scorers. There are several post moves that can be used in a given situation. A player who specializes in post moves will be able to quickly analyze the situation and know which move to use. Post players must develop some type of post game that allows them to consistently score in the post, especially if they are being heavily guarded by a defender. Many power forwards use a combination of this and the shooter scoring style.

The last scorer style is the slasher. Slashers put the ball on the floor and take their defender to the basket. Power forwards with large frames and height can have an advantage when driving to the goal against smaller players. Slashers also get fouled often, which can lead to easy points from the free throw line. This scoring style is most common among guard positions, although power forwards can still use it to great effect.

It is worth noting that players can and should incorporate all three scoring styles into their game. Doing so will greatly increase their offensive effectiveness and make them a threat to the opposing team.

Rebounder

The next style of play for the power forward position is the rebounder. This style describes a player that is known for his/her rebounding ability. These players are always boxing out when a shot is attempted and they try to get their hands on every rebound. Typically, this style of play is combined with other styles. It is rare to find a player that is only good at rebounding and nothing else.

Defender

The last style of play is that of the defender. Defenders are known to possess exceptional defensive capabilities that allow them to lock down opposing players on defense. Players that adopt this play style will attempt to limit the number of points made by the opposing team by any means. They will block shots, take charges, get steals, and contain players on defense. Quite a few professional players are known to adopt this style of play. They may not be very strong offensive players, but they make up for it on defense. Players will often receive plenty of playing time with this play style. Coaches love players that can play tough defense.

Combination

The final style of play is actually the most common. It is the combination of two or more different play styles. It is common because power forwards are, for the most part, skilled at more than one aspect of basketball. They are able to be great scorers, rebounders, and defenders all at the same time. There is really no limit to the skills and abilities that power forwards can add to their game. If you would like to become a well-rounded player, you should be constantly trying to add new abilities to your game. For example, if you're a strong scorer, you could attempt to be a strong defender as well and vice versa. You will in turn become more effective and revered for your abilities.

The Power Forward Position in a Nutshell

The main role of the power forward depends on the skill level of the individual player and what the team needs him/her to do. Traditionally, the power forward's main role is to assist the center in defending the painted area and rebounding in the paint. Power forwards also need to be able to score the ball and block shots. The power forward position is very important to a team's success because it is a tough and aggressive position. If you want to be an effective power forward simply remember to rebound and defend first, then add in other skills as you improve.

Center

Centers are considered to be a team's imposing presence in the paint. It is a position that is usually held by the team's tallest players. Centers are primarily responsible for defending the painted area, blocking or altering shots taken in the paint, and rebounding. They can also able to become offensive threats if they can use post moves or consistently make a 10 to 15-foot jump shot.

It's not uncommon for players at the center position to be 6-foot-10 or taller, especially at the professional level. Their height can give them a clear advantage when they are attempting to rebound or block shots. While height isn't that important for rebounding, it still comes in handy when attempting to grab the rebound in a crowd. There are other elements that factor into rebounding that I will discuss in the Rebounding chapter.

Centers should be able to score the ball in variety ways using post moves (like the drop step and hooks shot). However, the most common way for centers to score in the paint is to simply catch the ball and finish with a layup or dunk. They typically have the option of scoring in transition (if they can get back quick enough) or in a half-court setting. Traditionally, centers are supposed to play with their backs to the basket, but in recent years an increasing number of players have developed a face-up post game. Centers that only play with their backs to the basket are becoming fairly rare.

The center position is not considered to be as flexible as some of the other positions on the floor (though this largely depends on the skill level of the individual player). Defensively, centers will typically stay close to the basket, though they can venture out to the three-point line if necessary.

Since centers are expected to defend the paint, there are a few things that they can do to maximize their effectiveness. First, they need to keep opposing players out of the paint or at least make it difficult for them to cut through the lane. They can do this by either blocking their opponents' path or by using their body to give them a push/shove when they come through the lane. Second, they must be able to defend other post players in a one on one situation by playing tough defense. Lastly, they can use their strength to prevent the opposing center from backing them down in the paint.

Centers are also expected to be good rebounders. In fact, the center position may be the most important position for rebounding. This is because centers, more than even power forwards, are usually positioned near the goal where most rebounds tend to fall. Centers must box out and get inside position each time a shot is attempted so they can secure the rebound. This is especially crucial on defense, since defensive rebounds are the most important type of rebound.

Key Skills for Centers

There are multiple abilities that centers need to possess in order to be effective on offense and defense. These abilities include coordination and footwork, defensive ability, rebounding, the ability to catch the ball and finish at the rim, and the ability to use post moves. As you can see, there are many skills to discuss. Each of them is useful in its own way. I've already discussed rebounding and defensive ability at length so I'm going to only discuss them briefly in this section. However, I will go into a bit more detail regarding the other abilities.

Centers must possess good coordination and solid footwork to play to be effective. At this position, it's very easy to commit a travel by moving the wrong pivot foot or taking too many steps. Coordination and footwork will allow players to minimize this problem. Unfortunately, it's common for centers (especially taller centers) to be uncoordinated and have poor footwork. But, both of these abilities can be developed and improved upon. Footwork and coordination can open up several options for centers in the post. On offense, they will be able to take advantage of more advanced post moves. On defense, they will be able to slide their feet to contain their defensive matchup. In short, good coordination and solid footwork should be the foundation of a center's game.

Defensive ability and rebounding are two of the most important abilities for this position. Centers must be able to defend opposing players in and out of the paint. They must be able to block or alter any shots taken around the basket and help if an offensive player drives to the lane. It is also very important that they rebound the ball. Each time a shot is attempted (either on offense or defense), the center needs to box out and try to grab the rebound. Centers should attempt to grab every rebound they can get, especially those that land in or around the paint. Both of these skills can be improved through practice and experience.

Lastly, centers need to be able to catch the ball, use post moves, and finish strong at the rim. One of the first skills that need to be developed on offense is the ability to catch the ball. This may seem like an easy task, but some players still seem to struggle with it. Players at this position must have soft hands to be able to catch quick passes from teammates. Centers need to be able to use post moves to score when they receive the ball in the post. There are several post moves that a center can learn, but the most important two will likely be the drop step and hook shot. Finally, centers need to be able to finish strong. The other two offensive abilities mean nothing without the ability to finish a play. This may mean powering through one or more defenders or drawing a foul. The post player that is able to catch the ball, make a move, and finish the play will be a huge benefit for his/her team.

Additional Skills

The other skills that centers can possess (but are not required) are ball-handling, shooting, and passing ability. These three skills can have a tremendous impact on the overall ability of a center.

Ball-handling can make it easier for centers to avoid defensive pressure. They can simply dribble to a new location or around a defender. It will also help them create open shot opportunities or attack the basket. There aren't too many players at this position that can dribble the ball, so players that can will definitely set themselves apart. Another added benefit is that the center will be able to assist the guards in breaking the press. Imagine how beneficial it would be to have a center that could relieve some of the pressure from a full-court press.

Shooting ability is another skill that can improve a center's offensive game. If a center is able to shoot from 15 feet, it forces the defense to play closely and spaces out the floor. Good shooting ability will also make it easier to pump fake a defender. Defenders will often fall for the pump fake if they believe that the shooter can make the shot. This will give the shooter an opportunity to pass by the defender and score the ball. Shooting ability is a great skill to add to any player's game.

Passing ability can allow centers to make good passes to teammates from the post or to start a fast break. For example, centers can pass the ball to a teammate that is cutting to the basket or sprinting down the court. Centers that can pass the ball are a great benefit to their team because they keep the offense running smoothly. The idea is for the defense to collapse on the center position when the ball is passed down low. Then, that player will pass the ball back out to a teammate on the perimeter for an open shot. This pass must be quick and on target, which is why passing ability is so important for this position. Occasionally, players on the opposite side of the lane will cut to the goal and get open. The center needs to be able to see them and make a good pass for a quick scoring opportunity. Passing ability is important at this position and can benefit the team by adding a new dynamic to the offense.

Centers can add each of these skills to their game to become more well-rounded players. While it is not necessary to possess every skill, players should still attempt to develop most of them. How much the center will actually use these skills depends on the player and the needs of the team.

Styles of Play

The styles of play for the center position are similar to that of the power forward position, with a few differences.

Scorer

The scorer style of play is actually quite common for this position. Many centers are strong scorers and are able to score the ball in a variety of ways. However, they must call for the ball on offense so that their teammates know they want it. Scorers can be broken up into categories that include post moves, shooters, and finishers (or a combination of all three).

The use of post moves is a very common way to score down low. Players may use a hook shot, up-and-under, or even a drop step move to score the ball against a defender. There are numerous post moves that can be added, memorized, practiced, and used in a game; each with their own level of effectiveness. Many players may feel the need to utilize many different moves, but in reality, only a handful of moves are really necessary.

The next scoring style is the shooter. Centers who are shooters have a range of at least 10 to15 feet, but unlike the shooter scoring style of other positions, they typically don't have three-point range. These players do most of their shooting around the free throw line and short corner. When this scoring style is combined with post moves, centers suddenly have an offensive game that is very difficult to stop. Centers should also try to develop a consistent shot so they can lure defenders out of the paint. This will open up the lane for other players to drive and cut to the goal.

The final scorer style is the finisher. Finishers receive the ball around in the paint and perform either a layup or a dunk. They can receive the ball in transition, with a hand-off, with an alley-oop, or by receiving a pass in a half-court offense. Finishers need to keep their hands up and ready to catch the ball. They also need soft hands to catch quick passes and coordination to finish plays without traveling. Finishers are the most common way for centers to score in the post.

Rebounder

The next play style is the rebounder. Centers are expected to grab rebounds in and around the paint. Since these players are expected to be rebounders, they need to work on and improve this aspect of their game. The coaches and the team will appreciate a center that is able to rebound the basketball consistently. Rebounding shouldn't be thought of as a style of play for this position. It should be thought of as a mandatory extension of the scorer or defender style of play.

Defender

The last style of play is the defender. Centers should be and are actually expected to be good defenders. They must defend the lane and stop opposing players from getting to the rim. They need to block, or attempt to block, any shots that are attempted in the paint. They must also be able to stop opposing centers from scoring in the post. Defenders are a great asset to their team, especially if the opposition focuses on driving to the basket or scoring in the paint.

All of these play styles should be combined and added to a center's game. Players that are able do all of these things will be a threat on both offense and defense. They will get plenty of playing time and the coaches will appreciate their abilities. However, they must continuously develop all their abilities to become the best they can be.

The Center Position in a Nutshell

As I've mentioned throughout this section, the main role of a center is to defend and rebound. They must make it their mission to box out and to keep other players from scoring in the paint. If you would like to be a great center, just make sure to do these two things extremely well. The center position may not be as flexible as other positions, but that doesn't mean that it's not important on both ends on the floor. In fact, some teams are built around the center position. Some coaches will plan their offensive and defensive strategies around these players.

Chapter 3 | Basic Offensive Techniques

*"You can't get much done
in life if you only work on the
days when you feel good."*
– Jerry West

What are Offensive Techniques?

Offensive techniques are used to get in position to make a play, advance past a defender to score, or to get a slight advantage over the defense. They can also be used strategically to cause a defender to foul. The techniques listed in this chapter are basic, but they can also be very useful.

There are many different types of offensive techniques, such as the jump stop, pump fake, and jab step. Each of these techniques is effective in certain situations. For instance, the jump stop can be used to get past a defender when driving to the goal. Offensive players typically use it just before they get into the paint. The pump fake is used to make a defender jump into the air. Once the defender does so, the offensive player can move to get a clear shot at the goal. It is also likely that the defender will foul the offensive player in the process, which is an added bonus. The jab step can be used to get a defender off-balance so that the ball-handler can drive to the goal. It can be very effective against defenders that are playing up close and it may cause them to foul. The point is that all basketball techniques are different and have their own strengths and weaknesses.

Some offensive techniques require certain skills to be performed correctly. First of all, you will need to practice the techniques to improve your familiarity with them. The more you practice, the easier the techniques will be to use when you need them. Second, you will need a certain amount of coordination to perform the techniques. Good hand-eye coordination is necessary to perform a move or technique quickly enough to fake out a defender. Third, you will need solid footwork to use any offensive techniques. For example, the jump stop and euro step both require specific footwork to avoid committing a traveling violation. Lastly, agility is needed to use the offensive techniques to get past defenders. Of course, you don't have to be the most coordinated or have the best footwork to perform any these techniques. However, developing your physical abilities will help you to become more effective with them.

Techniques with the Basketball
Triple Threat Stance

The triple threat stance is a stance in which the ball-handler can quickly pass, shoot, or dribble the ball. It is recommended that players get into this stance whenever they receive the ball out on the perimeter or three-point line. It is a very versatile technique because it prepares the ball-handler to quickly make any number of offensive plays. The ball-handler will be able to react to what the defender is doing and make a play. To get into the triple threat stance, start with the ball in both hands and your feet slightly wider than shoulder width apart. Bend your knees, lean forward, and move the ball to either side of your body. From this position, players can jump straight up to shoot the ball, quickly pass it to a teammate, or take a defender off the dribble.

There are three total positions to the triple threat stance: one with the player's body facing toward the goal and the ball tucked to one side, one with the ball over the player's head, and the last with the player's body facing slightly away from the goal.

Pivots

Pivoting allows players to square up to the goal, turn their backs to it, or face a teammate. When players are in possession of the ball, they are only allowed to move one foot without taking a dribble. The other foot will become their designated pivot foot. If the ball-handler moves both feet without first taking a dribble, it will result in a traveling violation.

Players can use the pivot to create space between them and a defender. This is especially effective if the ball-handler's elbows are pointed outward while he/she is pivoting. It will force the defender move out of the way to avoid the elbow or risk getting hit by it. Just be sure not to throw an elbow at the defender or it will result in an offensive foul. Keep your arms stationary and just turn with your elbows pointed out.

Players can also add shoulder or ball fakes prior to pivoting to fake out the defense. These fakes can cause a defender to move in the wrong direction and create even more space for the ball-handler. For example, performing a fake before a pivot can be useful if you plan to shoot the ball. The defender should be unable to recover in time to contest the shot if he/she fell for the fake. A common technique is to fake left and then go right or vice versa.

To perform a pivot, begin with the ball in both hands and bend your knees. Then, decide which of your feet will be the pivot foot. Next, turn in the direction of that foot without lifting or sliding your pivot foot. For example, if you designate the right foot as the pivot foot, then you will turn to the right. Pivoting is a basic offensive technique that you will use constantly.

Reverse Pivot

The reverse pivot is another way to square up to the goal. It is very similar to a normal pivot except that it involves inverting the pivot by opening up in the opposite direction. To perform a reverse pivot, start with both hands on the ball, with your knees bent, and your back to the goal. To pivot left, make your left foot the pivot foot and turn clockwise until your body is squared up to the goal. To pivot right, make your right foot the pivot foot and turn counter-clockwise. The reverse pivot is a great way to face up to the goal if you ever receive the ball in the post or with your back to the basket. It will put you in a neutral position from which you can make any number of moves.

Jab Step

Jab steps are used to create room for the ball-handler by causing the defender to back off. They can also be used to fake out the defender by causing him/her to move in the wrong direction while attempting to guard you. They can keep the defender guessing and open up other options on offense. To perform the jab step, establish a pivot foot and move the other foot forward toward the defender. Ideally, the defender will shift his or her body in the direction that the jab was made. As soon as the defender shifts, you should have enough room to dribble past him/her, shoot, or pass the ball. Effective jab steps can leave defenders off-balance and make it difficult for them to recover to contest a play. Be sure to make the jab step look convincing. A good defender will not fall for a weak jab step, so make sure to sell it. Also, make sure to protect the ball while performing the jab so the defender will be unable to steal it.

You can also combine several jab steps together to create space between you and the defender. I will now discuss three different jab combinations that you can use to keep the defender off guard. First, you can jab step in one direction (causing the defender to shift in that direction) and then move in the opposite direction. As soon as the defender bites on the fake, lift the foot you used to jab with and step in the other direction. You can follow this combination with a pull-up jumper or a drive.

The second combination is to jab step in one direction and then continue in the same direction. The initial jab step should freeze the defender in place and allow you to move past him/her. This is a great follow-up move to the previous combination. The defender may be expecting you to move in the opposite direction and not see this move coming. This jab step combination will allow you to get a half step advantage on the defender, so I recommend using it to drive to the lane.

Lastly, you can jab into the defender to create space. This jab step should cause the defender to move backwards, which will free up enough room for you to take a shot or pass the ball. Be sure not to dip your shoulder into the defender when performing this jab step or it will be an offensive foul. Use your body to make contact with the defender.

Pump Fake

The pump fake is a faked shot attempt used to trick a defender into jumping into the air. If the defender bites on the fake, the ball-handler can take advantage by going to the goal or drawing a foul. This technique is particularly effective for situations in which the defender must run to contest a shot on the perimeter. In this situation, defenders will usually have to quickly lunge or jump at the shooter to have a chance at contesting the shot. If the shooter pump fakes, the defender will likely jump right past or end up fouling. To perform the pump fake, start your normal shooting motion, but do not jump or release the ball. Keep it in your hands and the defender should jump to contest or block it. When the defender is in the air, go past him/her or draw the foul. Try to look as natural as possible when performing the pump fake. Don't perform it too fast or slow.

Meeting the Ball

When receiving a pass from a teammate on the perimeter, you should step toward the ball prior to catching it. Meeting the ball in this manner can help limit turnovers resulting from intercepted passes. To meet the ball, run toward the pass as soon as it is released from your teammate's hands. Catch the pass just as the foot closest to the ball hits the ground. For example, if the ball were to your right, you'd catch the ball in stride on your right foot and vice versa for your left. It may take a bit of practice to get used to, but it does create a slight offensive advantage. It allows you to make a move as soon as the ball is caught.

Jump Stop

The jump stop is an offensive move in which the ball-handler picks up his/her dribble, jumps into the air, lands on both feet, and then jumps again to finish the play. The move is used to get past defenders and score close to the goal. To perform the jump stop, dribble toward the goal and pick up your dribble just before or immediately after getting into the lane. Jump into the air and land on both feet (making sure to guard the ball from defenders). Jump a second time toward the goal and finish the play with a layup or dunk. If there is a defender in front of you, try to jump around him/her with the initial jump and then jump toward the goal with the second jump. You must be sure to land on both feet at the same time after the first jump. If you land on just one foot and jump again, it will result in a traveling violation.

Euro Step

The euro step is a special type of move that precedes a layup or dunk. It involves stepping in two separate directions with each step after picking up your dribble. The move can be very effective in a one-on-one fast break situation or to get past taller defenders that are close to the goal. To perform the move, dribble toward the goal and pick up your dribble (as you would before a normal layup). Take one big step to the left or right, then immediately take another step in the opposite direction. If the defender tries to cut you off during the first step, you should go past him/her with your second step. After your second step, immediately perform a layup or dunk to finish the play.

Screens

Ball Screen

On offense, the ball-handler has the option to use a screen to get an open shot opportunity or to drive to the lane. Screens can be an effective way to free up an offensive player, especially if the defender doesn't see them coming. To set an on-the-ball screen, an offensive player will approach the defender guarding the ball-handler. The offensive player will then get low and block the defender's path. The ball-handler will dribble toward the screen and lead the defender into it. The defender should run directly into the screen and be temporarily taken out of the play, thereby freeing up the ball-handler to make an unguarded play. The ball-handler also has the option of not using the screen if the defender is overplaying or sees it coming. This is useful if the defender attempts to anticipate the screen by moving around it before it is actually set.

Off-the-Ball Screens

Screens that are set off the ball can free players up to receive a pass. Many offensive plays focus on setting screens off the ball. Offensive players can run a variety of routes around these screens to lose a defender and get open. A team's best shooters will often use off the ball screens to get an open shot opportunity because the defense is not likely to leave them open.

Back Screens

Back screens can be used to get an open path to the goal. Since the screens are set behind the defender, they are difficult to avoid, especially if the defender doesn't know they're coming. Back screens are one of the most effective types of screens because the defender will not be able to see the offensive player without turning his/her head. Set a back screen by standing behind the defender and angling your body so that the offensive player can head straight to the goal.

Setting Up the Defender

When an offensive player sets a screen, the receiver of that screen must set up the defensive player. To do this, the offensive player will walk in one direction with the defender close by. Then, that player will sprint toward the screen. The defensive player should run into the screen and the offensive player will be able to freely receive the ball to make a play.

Flare Out

The receiver of a screen doesn't always have to move toward the goal after using the screen. That player also has the option of going out to the perimeter or the three-point line to receive the ball. This is called a flare out and is a perfectly viable strategy to use (depending on what the defense is doing).

To perform a flare, set up the defender by walking him/her in a direction. When the screen is set, read the defender. If the defender gets hit with the screen or tries to anticipate it, pop out toward the perimeter and receive the ball for a shot. If the defender goes under the screen, you can pop out or backpedal in the opposite direction, away from the defender, to receive the ball. In both situations it will be difficult for the defender to recover in time to contest a jump shot.

Cuts

Cut

On offense, players will often move toward the goal with the intention of receiving the ball to score. The offensive player will set the defender up by walking or jogging in one direction and then sprinting toward the goal to receive the ball. The defender should be caught off guard by the change in direction and may have difficulty defending the play. Cuts are most useful when playing against a man-to-man defense, though they can still be used against a zone. Many teams make use of cuts to get quick points on offense.

Curl Cut

Curl cuts are best used when a defensive player is trailing the offensive player during a screen. The cutter will turn the corner (or curl) around the screen and head straight to the goal. Alternatively, the cutter can go around a screen and curl out to the perimeter for a shot opportunity. If the defenders switch on the screen, the screener should be able to pop out to get an open shot. Curl cuts are effective because they often force the defender to continue trailing behind the offensive player. If no other defender picks that player up then the cutter will have an easy layup or dunk.

V-Cut

This is a special type of cut in which the cutter's movements will form a "V" shape. The cut involves two different directions, one going away from the goal and the other toward the goal. Alternatively, the first direction can be toward the goal and the second can be away from the goal to receive the ball for a jump shot. The v-cut is effective because it allows the cutter to set the defender up then quickly change direction. To perform the cut effectively, start by walking or jogging in one direction. Then, plant one foot down, turn, and sprint toward the basket to receive the ball.

What's Next?

Throughout the next few chapters I will list some more specific offensive moves and techniques that involve shooting, ball-handling, passing, attacking the basket, and playing in the post. There is no limit to the number of offensive moves that you should know or use. However, your position will typically dictate the importance of learning one move over another. For example, point guards may use ball-handling moves and jump stops while power forwards may strictly use post moves.

Photo by Rick Yeatts

Chapter 4 | Shooting

> "The key to being a good
> shooter is balance.
> Everything follows balance."
> –Larry Bird

Why Shooting is Important

Shooting is the act of throwing the ball toward the goal in an attempt to get it through the rim. It is the method in which players score points so that their team can win a game. There are a wide variety of shots that players can use to score. A certain shot's level of effectiveness will largely depend on the situation it's being used in, as well as the skill level of the shooter.

Shooting the ball is one of the first skills that players should develop. It is also one of the skills that players should practice the most. Every player will have to shoot the ball at some point, so it's important that they know how to shoot it correctly. In the next section, I will list some basic and advanced shots. Mastering these shots will help you to get an advantage over the defense.

Basic Shots
Jump Shot

The jump shot is the most common shot in the game of basketball. It is a shot that can be taken anywhere on the court, but is mostly used outside of the painted area. The jump shot is good for elevating over a defender and getting a clear look at the goal. It also adds power to a shot without sacrificing accuracy.

To shoot a jump shot, stand with the ball in both hands and square your body up toward the goal. Your dominant hand should be on top of the ball and the other hand should be on the side of the ball. Then, place the ball in front of your body (around your midsection), bend your knees, and prepare to shoot. Jump into the air while simultaneously pulling the ball back toward your head, while bending your arm at the elbow. Your arm should form an L-shape with your elbow positioned under the ball. At the peak of your jump, release the ball and push it toward the goal. As the ball leaves your hand, the pointer or middle finger should be the last thing to touch the ball. Hold this position with your arm straight, wrist bent, and hand pointing toward the goal. Don't release this shooting position until the ball hits the rim or goes through the goal.

Set Shot

The set shot involves nearly the exact same form as a jump shot except that the shooter will stay on the ground instead of jumping. Set shots are typically only for free throws, though some players still use them while the ball is in play. I don't recommend using a set shot while being defended. It will become much easier for a defender to block the shot or make it difficult to see the goal. Players that use set shots are usually spot-up shooters that hang around the perimeter and wait to catch the ball. Players should shoot whatever shot works for them, but I highly recommend only using set shots for free throws.

Fadeaway

The fadeaway is a special type of jump shot in which the shooter leans back to avoid getting blocked by a defender. To perform a fadeaway, stand with your strong leg forward and weak leg back. For example, if you're right handed, your strong leg will be your right leg and your weak leg will be the left leg. With the basketball in your hands, push off your strong leg and jump back. You should be leaning back as you jump. Release the ball in the same manner as a normal jump shot. Add some arc on the shot so that the defender will be unable to block it. The fadeaway should not be used unless a defender is closely guarding you. Otherwise, it is best to use a regular jump shot.

Layup

A layup is a high percentage shot in which a player leaps toward the goal and uses resulting momentum to bounce the ball off the backboard and into the rim. It can be performed with either hand and on either side of the goal. If you don't use the backboard and shoot the ball underhanded then the layup is called a finger roll.

To perform a layup, start by dribbling toward the basket. Pick up your dribble just before you get to the paint, then take one or two steps toward the goal. Jump off the leg opposite of the hand you're going perform the layup with. Lastly, bounce the ball off the backboard or guide the ball into the rim. The hand that you use to perform the layup will depend on which side of the goal you're on and where the defenders are. Also, don't exceed two steps after picking up your dribble or it will be a traveling violation.

Defenders near the basket, especially post players, are the biggest obstacles when attempting a layup. These players may attempt to block the layup if they are nearby when it is attempted. You can avoid getting your layup blocked by using a different type of shot or layup, an offensive move, by moving the ball around the defender's arms prior to releasing the ball, or by drawing a foul.

Reverse Layup

The reverse layup is a variation of the normal layup. It involves performing the layup on the opposite side of the goal from where the shooter initially jumped. This layup allows players to use the rim and net as a barrier to prevent the defenders from reaching the ball. Reverse lay-ups are more difficult to perform than normal layups, but with practice, they can be made consistently.

Floater

The floater is a high arcing shot that is commonly used to get the ball over taller defenders in the paint. To shoot a floater, begin with the ball in both hands and then jump into the air. Use either hand to lightly push the ball upward toward the goal. When your arm is fully extended, release the ball. The shot should have enough arc to go over any defenders that attempt to block it.

Runner

The runner is very similar to the floater. The difference is that the runner will be performed while running toward the basket. The runner can be performed with one or both hands. To perform the shot, move toward the basket with the ball in both hands. Then, jump into the air using one leg and shoot the ball toward the goal. Make sure to shoot the ball lightly because your forward momentum will push the ball forward.

Free Throw

A free throw is a special type of set shot that occurs after a shooting foul is committed. The fouled player or, in the event of a technical foul, the chosen player is allowed one to three uncontested shots at the free throw line. This is one of the few times that a set shot should be used.

Free throws are arguably the most important type of shot in basketball. Making free throws is critically important to a team's success, especially in the later stages of a game. Players should make time to practice their free throw shooting whenever they can. I recommend shooting free throws at the end of your workouts to simulate the fatigue you'll feel during a game.

Good free throw shooting requires good concentration. Players must focus on making the shot and not on any of the distractions around them. The crowd will often try to distract shooters by making noises and gestures, so concentration is the key. When you shoot the free throw, be sure to keep your eyes focused on either the back or the front of the rim. Aim your shot to go just over the front of the rim or just short of the back of the rim. Many players perform some type of ritual before shooting a free throw. This is advisable because it gets you into the habit of doing the same thing each time you're at the line.

Shooting Tips

These are some tips that will allow you to improve your shooting accuracy and prevent your shot from getting blocked. These tips aren't specific to any position and every player should be able to find them useful. Each tip is easy to incorporate and make into a habit.

Hold the Ball in With Your Fingertips

When shooting, hold the ball with your fingertips. Don't allow the palm of your hand to touch the ball when shooting or it could alter your shot.

Focus on the Rim

While it is tempting to focus on the ball while shooting, try to look directly at the rim. Don't allow defenders or anything else to break your concentration; just focus on the rim. Looking at anything but the rim while shooting will lower your accuracy.

Follow Through

As you release your shot, follow through by flicking your wrist. When the ball leaves your hand, your wrist should bend and your fingers should point toward the ground. It should be as if you are trying to touch your forearm with your hand. Hold this position until the ball hits the rim or goes through the goal.

Aim

Point the last finger that touches the ball (the index or middle finger) toward the goal when releasing the ball to shoot. Try to imagine that you are putting that finger into the rim. Aiming will help to increase the accuracy of your shot.

Don't Shoot Flat

Make sure to add some arc on the ball when shooting. It will give the shot a better chance of being made as opposed to shooting it flat. Adding arc will also make the shot more difficult to block.

Don't Use Too Much Motion

Using too much motion on your shot may significantly affect your form and cause the shot to be off target. It can also increase the amount of time it takes you to get your shot off. Defenders can capitalize on this delay by closing in and blocking your shot. For example, putting the ball down too low or too far over your head is wasted motion. Shooting should involve a fluid motion and not a jerky one.

Don't Fade Unless Necessary

Fading away is a great offensive technique that you can use to get your shot off against tough defenders or shot blockers. However, it should only be used when necessary. If you're not being closely guarded, then there is no reason to use a fadeaway. Use your best judgment to determine if and when a fadeaway should be used.

Be Aware of Your Surroundings

Be aware of where the defenders are located on the court. If they are close enough to block or alter your shot, then you should use another strategy (like a pump or pass fake). Also, be especially wary of defenders that try to block your shot from behind. They can sneak up on you if you're not careful.

Add Range

It is important that you add range to your shot so you can be a threat all over the court. This is especially important for players at the guard positions, since they spend most of their time out on the perimeter. You can increase your shooting range through practice. Even centers can become good three-point shooters through training. I recommend starting close to the goal and gradually increasing the range of your shot until it extends to three-point range. Becoming a shooting threat will force the defense to play you closely and help to space out the floor.

Stay Ready

When awaiting a pass to shoot the ball, be sure to get into a shooting stance. This stance will lower the amount of time that it takes you to shoot the ball. To get into a shooting stance, bend your knees and face the player with the ball. Place your hands out in front of you and await the pass. As soon as you receive the pass, pivot, square up to the goal, and shoot. Being in this shooting stance will allow you to quickly shoot the ball before a defender can close out.

Final Thoughts

Becoming a good shooter is all about gaining muscle memory. In a game, you won't have time make sure all your shooting mechanics are perfect. You have to practice your shot until the mechanics are automatic. Shooting, especially free throw shooting, should be practiced whenever possible. Doing so will increase your shooting accuracy and consistency. To help with this, there are plenty of drills located in the Drills chapter toward the end of the book. You don't have to possess a picture-perfect shooting form, but you must use proper mechanics.

Chapter 5 | Ball-Handling

*"What to do with a mistake -
recognize it, admit it, learn
from it, forget it."*
– Dean Smith

What's Ball-Handling?

Ball-handling is the ability to control the basketball while dribbling. It is a skill that allows players to dribble around the court without losing control of the ball or having it stolen. Ball-handling is especially important for the guard positions because they will be in possession of the ball for most of the game. They will need solid ball-handling skills to bring the ball up the court, get past defenders, and drive to the basket. The ability to handle the ball also allows players to make use of ball-handling moves.

How to Dribble

To dribble, push the ball toward the ground with either hand. The ball will bounce and travel back up toward your hand. Meet the ball with left or right hand (with your palm pointing toward the ground) and repeat. You will continue to bounce the ball in this manner until you choose to pick it up. After picking up your dribble, you are only allowed to move on one designated pivot foot. Moving both feet will result in a traveling violation. If you resume dribbling after picking up the ball, it will result in a double dribble violation.

Who Should Dribble the Ball?

The answer to this question is simple. Each position is able to dribble the ball, but not every player possesses the skill necessary to handle the ball effectively. So, only players with solid ball-handling skills should dribble the ball, regardless of their position. However, there are only two positions in which ball-handling is a critical skill: the point and shooting guard positions.

Point guards handle the ball for the majority of a basketball game. They need excellent ball-handling ability to get the ball up the court against a defense. Point guards that lack this skill may become a detriment to their team because they will be susceptible to steals and traps.

Shooting guards need solid ball-handling ability to assist the point guard in bringing the ball up the court. It is especially important when the team is faced with a press defense. Players at this position that lack the ability to handle the ball may become liability on offense. They will become easier to defend and won't be able to create their own shots off the dribble.

The other positions on the court (the small forward, power forward, and center) don't necessarily need to have excellent ball-handling ability. But, these positions should develop some type of ball-handling skills to become more effective on offense. Doing so will make them more useful against a press defense and allow them to become bigger threats on offense. For example, post players that are able to handle the ball can become a serious matchup problem for the defense. They will be able to make moves off the dribble and create their own shot opportunities.

Tips to Improve Ball-Handling Ability

Keep Your Head Up

Be sure to keep your head up and your eyes off the ground, while dribbling. This will allow you to avoid defensive traps, limit turnovers, see open teammates, and make offensive plays. Players that look at the ground while dribbling struggle on offense because they aren't able to survey the court. Make a conscious effort to keep your head up while practicing your ball-handling skills. It may seem difficult at first, but with practice it will begin to feel like second nature.

Stay Low

Stay low to the ground while dribbling the basketball. It will increase your maneuverability and make it easier for you to protect the ball. You will also have more explosiveness and quickness. You won't have to bounce the ball as high or as hard, which will result in quicker, shorter bounces that are difficult to steal. A good rule of thumb is to keep the ball below waist-level while dribbling. That way you won't make the mistake of dribbling the ball too high.

Use Your Fingertips

Using your fingertips while dribbling will make it easier to control the ball. Dribbling with your palms will limit your ball-handling ability and make it difficult to use ball-handling moves. It is worth noting that nearly every action with the ball is performed with the fingertips such as shooting, dribbling, and passing.

Use Both Hands

You should be able to handle the ball with both hands. Doing so will give you more options while dribbling and make you more difficult to defend. Players that are unable to dribble with both hands will be put at a disadvantage. Defenders will force them to use their weak hand to dribble so they can steal the ball. Using both hands eliminates this vulnerability and will improve your overall offensive ability.

Protect the Ball

Always protect the ball when you're near a defender. Use your body as a barrier to keep defenders from reaching in and stealing the ball. This may cause the defender to make contact with you, which could result in a reaching foul. You may use your arms, shoulders, and hips to keep defenders from getting to the ball. Protecting the ball in this manner will help you limit your turnovers.

Alternate Your Speed

Changing up your speed while dribbling will put pressure on defenders in the open court. Speeding up and slowing down will force the defender to constantly change his/her defensive intensity. This should tire the defender out because it is difficult to play defense in this manner for an extended period of time. Alternate your pace and force the defender to try to keep up with you.

Dribble With a Purpose

Whenever you put the ball on the court, be sure to have a good reason for doing it. Don't dribble the ball just for the sake of it or you could get yourself into a bad situation. Once you begin dribbling, you'll eventually have to pick up the ball to pass or shoot. After that, you will no longer be able to put the ball on the floor or move both your feet. Only put the ball on the floor to move to a new location for a better scoring/passing opportunity or to get away from a defender.

Don't Pick Up the Dribble Without a Plan

To build upon the previous tip, don't pick up your dribble without a plan of action. If you do, you will have to remain in your current position until the ball is out of your hands. You will only be able to pivot, pass, or shoot from this position. The defense can take advantage of the situation by swarming you and attempting to force a turnover. Avoid getting into this trap by dribbling until you have an option for a play.

Become Comfortable With the Ball

You must become comfortable with the basketball to develop solid ball-handling ability. Otherwise, defenders will take advantage of your discomfort by attempting to force a turnover. Comfort with and confidence in your ball-handling ability can be attained through consistent practice. Perform ball-handling drills with a defender to simulate a game situation.

Don't Panic

A big part of ball-handling is avoiding turnovers. You can limit your turnovers by staying calm when you are in possession of the ball. The defense will attempt to rattle you to force a turnover, especially during traps. When you have the ball, remember to stay calm and make good decisions.

Use Ball-Handling Moves

Ball-handling moves can allow you to get past a defender in the open court, drive to the basket, or just get around a defender in a half-court offense. These moves can improve your offensive effectiveness, so it is important that you learn a few of them. However, try not to use too many moves at once. An initial move and a countermove (as a backup) should be all that is necessary.

__Ball-Handling Moves__

Crossover

The crossover move is one of the most basic ball-handling moves available. It's used to get past defenders by quickly changing directions. To perform the move, bounce the ball in front of your body from your right to left hand or vice versa. Plant your back foot on the ground and push off in the direction you want to go. Lift your opposite foot off the ground and move it past the defender. The defender should now be on the side of your body opposite the ball. Use your free arm to guard the ball from the defender. Continue moving past him/her and toward the goal.

During the crossover, do not dribble the ball too high or extend it too far out. Doing so will give defenders an opportunity to steal the ball. If you keep the ball low and close to your body, the crossover will be difficult to guard. The key is to keep the ball away from defenders so that they will be unable to reach in and steal it.

Be sure to move forward while performing the crossover as opposed to standing still. Attacking the defense will be much more effective than standing in one spot. There are variations to the crossover and an array of counter-moves that can make it even more difficult to defend. However, its effectiveness will still depend on the ball-handling skills of the player performing the move and the defensive ability of the defenders.

Between-the-Legs

The between-the-legs is another basic ball-handling move. It involves bouncing the ball between the legs to keep it away from a defender. The move is often used to get past defenders and attack the basket. To perform the move, bounce the ball between your legs so that it travels to the hand opposite of the defender. Your body should then act as a barrier between the defender and the ball. Use your lead foot to step past the defender while simultaneously pushing off with your back foot. If all goes well, this should give you at least a half a step advantage on the defender (which will open up additional options for you). If the move is performed correctly, it will be difficult for defenders to attempt a steal without fouling.

The between-the-legs can also be used to quickly change directions while dribbling since it moves the ball to your opposite side. Though the move is considered to be basic and simple, it can be very effective if used properly. However, like the crossover move, its effectiveness depends on the player's ball-handling skills and the defensive ability of the players on defense.

In-and-Out

The in-and-out is a ball-handling move that is used to trick a defender. The move fakes the crossover by keeping the ball in one hand instead of moving it from one hand to the other. To perform the in-and-out, move the ball in close to your body with one hand, then after the bounce, move it away from your body.

The defender should anticipate the crossover and end up moving away from the ball. This should give you enough room to go past the defender and move toward the goal. Be sure to bounce the ball hard and keep the ball so that the move can be made quickly. Also, be careful not to get a carrying violation when using the move.

Behind-the-Back

The behind-the-back move involves bouncing the ball behind your back to keep it away from defenders or to set up an additional move. To perform the behind-the-back move, bounce the ball behind your back from one side to the other. Then, step forward, past the defender, and move toward the goal to make a play.

You can think of this move as a crossover that is performed behind your back. It is one of the more difficult ball-handling moves to steal because your whole body acts as a barrier against the defender.

Wraparound

The wraparound is a variation of the behind-the-back move. Instead of bouncing the ball behind your back, you will use your arm to wrap the ball around your back. The ball should land and bounce on the opposite side of your body. To perform the move, place the ball in either hand and move it behind your back. Wrap your arm around your back toss it so that it bounces on the opposite side of your body. The ball should not hit the ground behind you. This move is useful for when you are running forward while being defended, especially if the defender attempts a steal.

Back Dribble

The back or retreat dribble is used to create space for the ball-handler so that he/she make a play. To perform a back dribble, stop just in front of the defender and take one or two step backwards (while maintaining your dribble). This should create enough room for you to shoot, pass, or make another play. The back dribble can also be used when advancing the ball up the court or to avoid a trap.

Spin Move

The spin move is a quick ball-handling move used to get past defenders. To perform the move, dribble the ball while moving forward and take a big step with the foot opposite the ball. Pivot on that foot and spin while holding on to the ball. This is a high level move that, if used quickly enough, should propel you right past the defender.

Killer Crossover

The killer crossover is a special type crossover. It is actually two separate moves performed one after the other. The first move is typically a crossover while the second move can be a between-the-legs, behind-the-back, or even another crossover. To perform the killer crossover, quickly perform a crossover and then immediately follow it with a second move. The idea is for the defender to commit to the crossover, but be unable to recover and stop the second move. This move should only be used when the initial move is unsuccessful. There should be no need to use two moves if the first one is successful.

Attack, Back Dribble, Drive

This is a combination of offensive moves that make up a counter-move. It is used to get past defenders to attack the basket. The goal of the move is to create an opening while the defender is trying to recover. These moves can be used if you are unable to get past the defender with the initial drive. The defender should back up on the play to cut off the driving lane. You can then perform a back dribble, which should cause the defender to step forward to recover. Lastly, dribble past the defender while he or she is recovering and head to the goal.

Chapter 6 | Passing

"Just play. Have fun. Enjoy the game."

– Michael Jordan

What's Passing?

Passing is the act of moving the basketball from one player to another on offense. It is a fundamental skill and one of the most important aspects of basketball. Understand that there is no specific position that should pass the ball. Every player on offense should be able to make basic passes to their teammates. However, players at the guard positions (the point and shooting guard) tend to be the best passers on a team.

Passing is all about precision, timing, and awareness. Passes need to travel directly to the recipient, unless they're intended to lead a player to the goal. An imprecise pass can lead to a turnover for the offensive team. However, using proper form can help to increase passing accuracy and limit these turnovers. Passes also need to be timed correctly. Passing to a player in motion is much more difficult than passing to one standing still. If the pass is made too early, it will go too far in front of the player. If it's made too late, it will go too far behind. Players should try to time their passes so they go directly to the player in motion.

Lastly, players must be aware of their surroundings when passing the ball. They must survey the court to see which teammates are open, which aren't, and where the defenders are located. Players that are open one second may not be open the next. It's important that the passer recognizes this and only makes a pass when a teammate is open.

Make sure that you don't telegraph your passes. Telegraphing means to make deliberate motions that indicate a certain action is about to be taken. Staring at the teammate you're about to pass to or slowly passing the ball are examples of telegraphing. Telegraphed passes will be easier for the defense to steal.

Some passes have a high degree of difficulty and take a certain amount of skill to perform. Poor passers shouldn't attempt to make difficult passes unless they are comfortable using them. With that said, each player should attempt to improve his or her overall passing ability for the benefit of their team. This can be accomplished by performing drills (like the ones listed in the Drills chapter) or through experience. Repetition and proper technique are the keys to becoming a great passer.

In the next section, I will list some basic passes that every player should know. Some of these passes may be better suited for certain situations than others. Be sure to use your best judgment when making a pass to a teammate.

Basic Passes

Chest Pass

A chest pass is a pass made at chest level. To perform the pass, start with both hands on the ball and hold it in front your chest. Push the ball out and away from your body with both hands toward the intended recipient of the pass. Both of your hands should point outward as the ball is released and your thumbs should point toward the ground. The chest pass is one of the most basic and commonly used passes in basketball. Players are able to add more strength to this or any pass by taking a step forward as they are making it. Doing so will add additional power and speed to the pass and make it much more difficult to intercept.

Chest Pass (One Hand)

This pass uses one hand to push the ball away from the chest, rather than two. To make the pass, start with both hands on the ball and hold it near your chest. Push the ball away from your chest with only one arm and make the pass. After the ball is released, your fingers should be pointing toward the ground. This pass can be made with either hand. Some players may find this pass to be more accurate than a normal chest pass, though it may not be as strong.

Bounce Pass

A bounce pass is performed in a similar manner to the chest pass. The difference is that this pass involves bouncing the ball off the court before the other player receives it. Bounce passes should be angled so that they don't bounce too high or low. They can be performed with one or two hands and at different angles. They are usually performed from the wing to the post or to a player moving toward the goal. Bounce passes are usually not to be used on the perimeter because they're slower than chest passes (which makes them susceptible to interceptions).

To make a bounce pass, hold the ball with both hands near your chest. Push the ball away from your body toward the ground and in the direction of your teammate. The ball should bounce off the ground and travel directly to him/her. Like the chest pass, your thumbs should point toward the ground after the ball is released.

Overhead Pass

This is a powerful, overhanded pass that can (for the most part) be used interchangeably with a chest pass. To perform the overhead pass, start with the ball in both hands and hold it over your head (Holding the ball up high in this manner can also keep it away from defenders). Then, pass the ball to a teammate by bringing your arms forward and releasing the ball. This pass uses more arm motion than a chest pass, which makes it even more powerful and quick. You can even use it to make long distance passes by taking a step forward as you release the ball. It is not uncommon for players to use this pass to get the ball down the court.

Baseball Pass

The baseball pass is a one-handed pass used to throw the ball long distances to a teammate. It is one of the most powerful passes available because it allows players to put their bodyweight into it. The pass can be very quick, so it's important to have some room between the passer and the recipient.

To perform this pass, start with the basketball in both hands. Then, move the ball into one hand and pull that arm back as if you're about to throw a baseball. Throw the ball toward a teammate using the necessary amount of strength. One of the pitfalls of this pass is that it is easy to over or under throw the ball (which could lead to a turnover). The baseball pass is typically not used in a half-court setting, though it can be if necessary.

Inbound Pass

An inbound pass is a pass made by a player that's out of bounds. This pass is usually made when a team gains possession of the ball after the opposing team scores, turns the ball over, or after a dead ball. The offensive player making the pass will only have five seconds to get the ball inbounded before a violation is called. Defenders may attempt to deny the inbound pass by impeding the passer's vision or by defending the potential recipients of the pass. The passer is allowed to run the length of the baseline after the opposing team scores or after a timeout that immediately follows the other team scoring the ball.

Lob Pass

The lob pass is a high arcing pass used to get the ball over the defense and to a teammate. Lob passes are typically used to get the ball to a player with inside post position. In this situation, a defender will be fronting the offensive player in the post. The ball will be lobbed over this defender to give the receiving player an open layup or dunk opportunity.

To perform the pass, push the ball away from your body at an upward angle. The pass should enough arc on it to float over the defenders. You should be careful when using this pass, as it is slower than many of the other passes. Defenders can and will try to intercept the pass if it is used in the wrong situation.

Alley-oop Pass

An alley-oop is a special type of lob pass. The player receiving the ball will catch the ball in mid-air and finish with a layup or dunk. This pass requires good timing by the passer and the receiver to be completed successfully. Alley-oops are often the end result of a fast break (with at least two offensive players), a back screen (in a half-court setting), or a cut to the goal (in a half-court setting). A successful alley-oop is one of the most exciting plays in the game of basketball.

To perform the pass, hold the ball in both hands and wait until you see your teammate moving toward the goal. When that player gets near the paint, lob the ball toward the goal. Be sure not to pass the ball too high or too low or it can result in a turnover. Try to get the ball as close to the rim as possible so the receiver can catch it and finish.

Advanced Passes

Behind-the-Back Pass

The behind-the-back pass is a pass that's made behind the passer's back. This pass, and some of the other advanced passes, have a higher degree of difficulty than the basic passes. With that said, a certain amount of skill is necessary to make the behind-the-back pass correctly. The ball must be released at the right angle and the right time to make it to the intended recipient. This pass can trick the defender and make it difficult for him/her to anticipate where the ball will be passed.

To make the pass, start with both hands on the ball. Then, quickly move the ball behind your back with one hand. Release the ball as your arm moves further around your back. The ball should travel directly to your teammate to complete the play. The behind-the-back pass can be made with either hand and as a bounce pass.

No-Look Pass

No-look passes make it difficult for the defense to anticipate where the ball will be passed. Good defenders usually watch the ball-handler's eyes to see where a pass is going. If the ball-handler telegraphs the pass by looking directly at its recipient, the defender may attempt a steal. The no-look pass eliminates this vulnerability because the passer doesn't look directly at the intended recipient. This prevents the defender from anticipating the pass trajectory and attempting a steal. A defender may still be able to predict a pass, but it will be difficult. To throw a no-look pass, simply look away from the intended target and pass the ball.

Jump Pass

The jump pass is a pass that's made in mid-air. This is a dangerous pass because the passer must get the ball to a teammate before touching the ground. If there is no other player open to receive the ball, then it can result in a turnover. There are several situations in which this pass could end badly. However, many professional players still use it. My personal recommendation would be to stay on the ground while you're passing the ball unless it is absolutely necessary.

Layup to Pass

This pass is used when a player believes that his/her shot will be blocked while performing a layup. That player will pass the ball to a teammate with a better scoring opportunity. Depending on the situation, this pass can lead to a wide-open shot attempt. However, there is some risk involved with this pass. A defender could easily intercept the ball or the passer could be passing up a good scoring opportunity. Also, like the jump pass, the player will have to pass the ball before touching the ground or a violation will be called. To perform the pass, drive to the goal and begin perform a layup. Then, while in midair, pass or hand the ball off to a teammate to finish the play.

Off-the-Backboard Pass

The off-the-backboard pass is a trick play in which the ball is bounced off the backboard to a teammate. It's typically not a pass that's used for competitive play. However, the pass is legal and can result in a crowd-pleasing finish if it's executed successfully. The pass can be made from one player to another or one player can toss the ball to himself/herself. Like the alley-oop, this pass can be exciting to watch.

Pass Fake

A pass fake is an offensive technique in which the player, in possession of the ball, makes a motion to pass but does not release the ball. The pass fake is used to fool a defender into thinking a pass is going to be made. The defender should shift in the direction of the fake, which will allow the ball-handler to make a move or shoot. The pass fake can help to break a press, get the ball to an open player, or get the defense to shift in a way that is beneficial to the offense. Pass fakes can even open up opportunities to make better passes. For example, a guard could make a pass fake (high or low) before passing the ball into the post to catch a defender off-guard. The defender should shift and leave enough room to make an entry pass into the post. Pass fakes work well on defenders that like to get into the passing lanes and get steals. This pass is an important offensive tool that can keep the defense on its toes.

Pass Fake to Layup

This is a variation of the layup to pass. A fake is made just before attempting the layup. It is used to trick defenders into thinking a pass is going to be made instead of a layup. This will cause them to move to deflect the pass or attempt to defend the intended recipient of the pass. The ball-handler should be left with an open path to the goal. The pass fake must look convincing if you want a defender to fall for it. It cannot be made too fast or too slowly.

Behind-the-back Pass Fake to Layup

The behind-the-back fake to layup is another layup to pass variation. The offensive player will fake a behind-the-back pass, and then attempt a layup. Ideally, the fake will fool the defender and cause him/her to move out of the way, leaving an open path to the goal. This move can be used to get easy points in transition.

Chapter 7 | Attacking the Basket

*"I tell kids to pursue their
basketball dreams, but I tell them to
not let that be their only dream."*
– Kareem Abdul-Jabbar

Why Attack the Basket?

Attacking the basket is one of the most common ways to score the ball on offense. Offensive players will drive to the basket when there is an open lane to the goal or when a poor defender is guarding them. The point guard, shooting guard, and small forward are usually the players that attack the basket. These positions are able to drive to the goal because they're often positioned out on the perimeter. Post players don't usually drive to the goal, but it is not that uncommon for them to do so.

A drive to the basket can end in a few different ways. It could end positively with the ball-handler attempting to score or pass the ball. Or, it could end negatively with the ball-handler committing an offensive foul or turning the ball over. The most common way to end a drive is with some type of shot. Common shots include layups (the most common), floaters, and pull-up jump shots. The type of shot that is used by the ball-handler will depend on the situation. The ball-handler must analyze what the defenders are doing, and then decide which shot to use. Passing the ball to finish a drive is another valid option. The ball-handler can pass the ball if he/she is unable to make it to the basket or if a scoring opportunity is not available. He/she can pass the ball out to a teammate with a better shot opportunity. Driving to the basket is also an effective way to attract additional defenders, which will leave other offensive players open. Identifying the help defense and passing to an open teammate can lead to a great offensive opportunity. Keep in mind that you should only pass the ball when you don't have a clear shot of your own. Don't pass up a good scoring opportunity to give the ball to another player who may not have a better shot. Assess the situation and use your best judgment. A defensive foul could be called on the defender if the ball-handler draws contact during the drive or the finish. This could put the offensive player on the free throw line for some easy points. Try to draw a foul during the drive to get the opposing team in foul trouble and to get a chance at the free throw line.

A drive ends negatively if an offensive foul is called or a turnover is made. Both of these outcomes hurt the team and will lead to the opposing team gaining possession of the ball. A common offensive foul committed during a drive is the charging foul. This occurs when the ball-handler runs into a defensive player while that player's feet are set. The result will be a lost possession and the ball will be awarded to the opposing team. The common causes of turnovers during a drive are missed passes, a loss of possession, and steals. A turnover also results in a wasted possession and the ball will be given to the opposing team. Slow down and protect the ball to avoid these mistakes.

Attacking the basket can be broken up into separate, important elements: players should stay low, guard the ball from defenders, go around the defenders, stay on balance, and finish the play. All of these elements build upon each other so that you can perform the drive properly.

Tips for Attacking the Basket

Stay Low

Staying low will increase your speed and make it easier to control the ball without turning it over. Being upright slows you down and makes it easier for defenders to stop the drive. As soon as you take your first step to begin the drive, stay as low as possible until the play is completed.

Guard the Ball

When you are driving to the basket, defenders will attempt to tip the ball out of your hands. Use your body and arm as a barrier to protect the ball from defenders. Keep them at bay and keep the ball safe.

Go Around the Defender

The next element is to step around the defender. This may seem obvious, but it is easy to forget in the moment. If you dribble straight into the defender, you have a greater chance of committing a turnover or a charging foul. Move around the defender with your initial step. Try to get the defender behind you or on your hip while moving toward the goal. Getting the defender in one of these positions will increase the chance that he/she will commit a defensive foul. If you have trouble getting around the defender, then you may have to use a ball-handling move first.

Utilize angles to score and pass the ball. For example, you can drive to the basket at an angle and use the backboard to assist in scoring a layup. It may also help you to locate an open teammate.

Stay on Balance

Stay on balance when driving to the lane or you may not be able to make it to the goal. Being off balance may cause you to fall or make it difficult for you to score the ball.

Finish

Lastly, you want to finish the play. Either attempt to score the ball or pass it to an open teammate. Just try to finish the play on a positive note.

Common Mistakes

There are a few things that can go wrong when attacking the basket. Use the following three tips to help limit those mistakes. First, don't dip your shoulder into a defender when driving to the goal. This will result in an offensive foul and the ball will be awarded to the opposing team. You are allowed to use your body to block off the defender, but you cannot dip your shoulder. Second, refrain from pushing the defender away. It may be tempting to push the defender to get a better look at the goal, but it will result in an offensive foul. Use your arm to block off the defender, but do not push off. Lastly, don't expose the ball. Exposing the ball gives the defender an opportunity to tip the ball away, which can result in a turnover. Keep the ball close to your body as you're moving toward the basket.

Also, try not to overextend your arms so the ball won't be vulnerable to steals. Keep all of these tips in mind when attacking the goal to minimize turnovers and mistakes.

Chapter 8 | Playing in the Post

"I treated it like every day was
my last day with a basketball"
– LeBron James

The Positions, Responsibilities, and Flexibility of Post Players

The power forward, center, and occasionally the small forward are considered to be post positions. These players spend most of their time in or around the paint. Their responsibilities typically include scoring around the basket, rebounding, defending the paint, and blocking/contesting shots.

Post players have a great amount of flexibility when it comes to scoring the ball. They have the option of scoring with their backs to the basket, with a jump shot, or with a layup in transition. They also have several post moves that they can use to score against a defender such as the drop step, hook shot, and turnaround jumper. However, these players must be able to play physically or they will not be effective. They must be able to use their size and strength to dominate their position.

How to Post Up

In the post, defenders will often try to front the offensive player or use one arm to deny an entry pass. Posting up allows the offensive player to get and maintain position so that he/she can receive the ball. To post up, stand just above the block and squat down with a wide stance. Your legs should be a little more than shoulder width apart. Use one arm to block off the defender and the other one as a target for the pass. Your target hand will allow the passer to see where you want the ball to be passed. For example, you could hold your hand high for a lob pass or low for a bounce pass.

Use your lower body and arms to keep the defender behind you. If the defender tries to move in front, slide your feet to maintain contact. Maintaining contact in this manner will make it difficult for the defender to get back in front of you. Don't use your arms to hold onto the defender, or it will be an offensive foul. Just block the defender off with your arms without holding.

What Should a Post Player Do When the Ball is Received?

When a player receives the ball in the post, his/her next move will depend on a few factors: what the defense is doing, where they are on the court, and their individual skill level. The defense is able to guard the post position in many different ways. They can stand behind the post player, three quarter deny, or front the post. Post players should read the defense before and upon receiving the ball so they can assess the situation. The post player's location is the next important factor. If the player catches the ball underneath the goal, the he or she should perform a layup or dunk. If the ball is caught around the free throw line, then a jump shot or drive may be the best course of action. If the post player gets the ball in the post, then a post move may be the way to go. It all depends on where the post player is positioned in the offense. Finally, skill level is one of the most important factors in determining what a post player should do after receiving the ball. Some players are best with their back to the basket, while others prefer to face up. Post players should use whatever moves and techniques they're most comfortable with to get the best results. I recommend mastering at least three post moves so that you can be ready in any situation.

Moves in the Post

Post moves are moves that are performed in the post against a defender (usually in a one-on-one situation). These moves are usually reserved for the post positions, but any player can use them. The moves can be very effective against the defense if used in the right situation. For example, if a defender is overplaying on one side, a power dribble may allow you to get to the goal with ease. Every post move has some type of counter move that can be used to keep the defense guessing. Remember to read the defense before you make a move. The post moves section will be split into two categories: post techniques and basic moves.

Post Techniques

Power Dribble

The power dribble is a hard, two-handed bounce that players can use to get closer to the goal. It can be used to get past defenders in the post or to knock them off-balance. The bounce will be difficult for defenders to steal because of its power and speed. To perform a power dribble, get low and bounce the ball with both hands. The dribble should be low and hard so that it can quickly bounce back into your hands. The power dribble should be used in conjunction with the drop step to move toward the goal. This technique should only be used around the basket. It's not practical to use anywhere else on the court.

Back Down

Backing down a defender in the post is a great way to get closer to the goal. The technique allows players to use their bodies to force a defender to move backwards. The purpose of the technique is to get closer to the goal for an easier shot attempt. To use the back down, bounce the ball while simultaneously bumping into the defender with your body. Typically, the technique is only to be used against a man-to-man defense. Don't use the technique against a double team or help defense. Also, be sure not to dip your shoulder into the defender; it will result in an offensive foul. While performing the technique, defenders may try to cause you to lose your balance. You can avoid this by not leaning on the defender.

Look Fake

The look fake is a special type of fake in which a player looks in a particular direction to fool a defender. The defender will believe that you're going in that direction and move to defend. Then, the player will pivot or spin in the opposite direction and score the ball.

Basic Moves

Hook Shot

The hook shot is a short-range, one-handed shot used to score in the post. It allows the shooter to use his or her body as a barrier to block the defender. The ball is shot across the shooter's body with his/her outside hand. If performed correctly, the hook shot can be very difficult to block. To perform the move, catch the ball in the post and pivot on either foot. Turn your body so that your shoulder is perpendicular to the goal. This shoulder will be used to block off the defender. Jump and shoot the ball across your body, while using your inside arm to block off the defender.

You can take one to two dribbles prior to shooting the hook shot. This can allow you to get closer to the goal or set up an additional move. The hook shot can also be banked off the backboard if you use the proper angle. Shooting off the backboard in this manner can occasionally provide you with an easier shot. The hook shot is a move that every post player should try to master. It will come in handy in many different situations.

Drop Step

The drop step is a powerful, long step toward the goal. The move is used to get around defenders to score the ball in the post. To perform the drop step, catch the ball in the post and step toward the goal with either leg. Your leg should wrap around one of the defender's legs (this should give you a path to the goal). Continue moving the rest of your body (around the defender) in the direction of the step. Square up to the goal and perform a layup to finish the play. Try to perform the move so that you end up in front of the goal and not directly under it. Be sure to chin the ball as soon as you catch it and keep it there for the duration of the move. You can combine the power dribble with the drop step if you need to, but it is not always necessary. The drop step is an important move that every post player should master.

Turnaround Jumper

The turnaround jumper is a basic move used to shoot over the top of a defender. If performed quickly enough, the move can be difficult to defend. To perform the move, catch the ball in the post and pivot on either foot. Then, rise up and shoot the ball over the top of the defender. Don't shoot the ball until your body is facing the goal. If a defender is playing closely, then you can use a ball or shoulder fake prior to taking the shot. These fakes can allow you to get a clearer shot at the goal. Fadeaways can also be used if you're playing against a taller player. The fadeaway can give you more space to get your shot off, but it may make the shot more difficult.

Up-and-Under

The up-and-under is a counter move for the turnaround jumper. The move is used to get the defender into the air so that the shooter can get an open path to the goal. The up-and-under consists of a pivot, pump fake, and a step toward the goal. To perform the up-and-under, catch the ball in the post and pivot on either foot. Square up to the goal and perform a pump fake. The defender should bite on the fake and jump into the air. Step past the defender with your non-pivot foot and move toward the goal. Jump and perform a layup to finish the play.

Be sure to perform the pump fake at the right speed. The fake shouldn't be made too fast or too slowly. Try to mimic a natural shooting motion. You also have the option to take a dribble after performing the pump fake to get closer to the goal. The up-and-under can be an extremely useful move that can get you easy points in the post.

Spin-Off

The spin-off is effective move to use when a defender is leaning or pushing against you. It uses the defender's momentum and aggressiveness to your advantage. To perform the move, post up above the block with the defender behind you. You should be in a low stance, with your knees bent and your arms out. As soon as you receive the ball, pivot and spin off the defender. You should then have an open look at the goal for a layup. The move should be performed quickly so that it catches the defender off-guard. The spin-off can be performed in either direction and combined with a hook shot or turnaround jumper.

Look Over Shoulder, Then Spin

Start at the top of the block and catch the ball in the post. Look over your left or right shoulder and spin in the opposite direction. This move should cause the defender to shift in the direction that you initially looked. This move builds upon the spin move and can be used to keep the defender guessing.

Face Up Sweep-through

The sweep-through is a move that can be used in the post and on the perimeter. It is a move that must be performed quickly to be effective against a defender. To perform the move, post up on the block with a defender behind you. Catch the ball and perform a reverse pivot. As soon as your body is squared up to the goal, sweep the ball low in front of your body. You will then take a long step past the defender, which should open a path to the goal. The direction of the sweep through will depend on the direction of your pivot. If you pivoted with your left foot, then you will sweep through from left to right (and vice versa for the right foot).

Combining moves and dribbling

It's common to take one or two dribbles before performing any of these moves. Dribbling the ball can help you to get better position or set up a move. Players can also combine moves together if they need to. Below are a few examples to illustrate how this can be accomplished.

Two-dribble Drop Step

Start on the block and receive the ball. Take two dribbles to the left or right, then drop step toward the goal. Wrap the leg you're stepping with around the defender's legs while performing the move.

Two-dribble Drop Step to Hook Shot

Start above the block and receive the ball. Take two dribbles to the left or right, and then perform a drop step in the opposite direction. Perform a hook shot over the defender to finish the play. This move uses the drop step to get better position to make the hook shot.

Two-dribble Pump Fake

As with the previous moves, start on the block and receive the ball. Take two dribbles to the left or right then perform a pump fake. The defender should jump into the air to attempt a block. As soon as the defender is in the air, step through and perform a layup. This move is a little more deceptive than the previous ones. The defender will expect you to shoot the ball as soon as you pick up your dribble. A well-timed shot fake should allow you to get an open shot.

There are even more combinations that you could try. For example, you could take two dribbles, drop step, pump fake, and then perform a hook shot. There may be a time when you need to combine more than two or three moves together, but this should be rare. Usually, you will only need one or two moves to be successful in the post.

Chapter 9 | Rebounding

*"Push yourself again and
again. Don't give an inch until
the final buzzer sounds."*

– Larry Bird

What is Rebounding?

Rebounding is the act of securing the ball after a missed shot. It is one of the most important aspects of basketball and has a serious impact on the outcome of a game. The team that controls the boards will control the game. Good rebounding teams can limit the opposing team's second-chance opportunities and create additional opportunities for themselves. Every player on a team should be able to (at least) rebound on the defensive end of the floor.

Who is Expected to Rebound?

Post players are expected to be the main rebounders for a team. These players are usually positioned near the goal, where most rebounds occur. However, post players aren't the only positions that can rebound the ball. Guards and wing players can also become good rebounders. These players should, at the very least, be able to box out and rebound on defense.

Any player can become a great rebounder through effort. It is the most important characteristic for rebounding.

How to Rebound

To rebound the ball effectively, players must box out when a shot is attempted. To box out, position your body between the goal and the opposing. Keep this player behind you by using your lower body to make contact. Failing to box out will give the opposing team a better opportunity to collect the rebound. When a shot is attempted, immediately find the closest player from the opposing team and box out.

Every player should box out and rebound on defense. However, this isn't always true on offense. Sometimes, guards will get back on defense as soon as a field goal is attempted to stop fast breaks.

Rebounds can be separated into two categories: offensive and defensive.

Offensive Rebounds

Offensive rebounds are rebounds that are secured by the offensive team. This type of rebound gives the team a second chance to score the ball after the initial shot is missed. Players can grab an offensive rebound to perform a put back or to restart the offense. Restarting the offense is an effective way to tire out the defense because it forces them to defend for an extended period of time.

Offensive rebounds can also be secured after free throw attempts, but the offensive team will be at a disadvantage. The defenders will automatically have inside position because of the way players are positioned during a free throw. However, if the offensive player is quick enough he/she can still secure the rebound. When the ball is released, the offensive player must quickly slide in front of the defender and box out. But not every player needs to go after the offensive rebound. Most teams send one or two players back on defense to prevent a fast break.

Defensive Rebounds

Defensive rebounds are rebounds secured by the defensive team. They are also the most important type of rebound. Failing to secure the rebound on defense could be disastrous. The opposing team could get a second opportunity to score the ball.

Defensive rebounds are also the most common type of rebound. These rebounds are easier to secure because the defense usually has inside position. They can easily turn, box out, and grab the rebound. The defense also has the inside position when the opposing team is shooting free throws. The defensive player can easily step in front of the offensive player and box out.

Rebounding Techniques

When a shot is attempted, players can use any of these techniques to get better position. Their usefulness will depend on the situation and how the opposing player reacts.

Box Out

Boxing out will greatly increase your chances of securing a rebound. Each time a field goal is attempted, you should box out the closest player from the opposing team. It should be your goal to keep the other team from getting the rebound. Be sure to make the initial contact with the other player before you box out.

Swim Move

The swim move is a technique used to get in front of an opposing player. It is useful for both posting up and rebounding. The move involves the use of both arms to move an opposing player backwards. You will have the opportunity to get position as the player is moving backwards.

To perform the swim move, take your outside arm and move it in front of the opposing player's chest. Push the player toward you while simultaneously bringing your inside arm over the player's head. Now, step in front of the player to get position. As soon as you're in front of your opponent, get low and hit him/her with your lower body. Maintain contact until you jump to grab the rebound. Remember that the move has three steps: use your outside arm to push the opposing player backwards, move your inside arm over his/her head, and step in front. Your arms should make a swimming motion when you're performing the move.

Spin-Off

The spin-off is a technique used to get inside position or good post position. It uses the momentum of your body to knock an opposing player off-balance. You will get the opportunity to get position while the other player is trying to regain balance. The technique uses the weight of your body against the opposing player. To perform the technique, plant one foot in between the opposing player's feet. Then, pivot so that the backside of your lower body makes contact with the opposing player. As you pivot, get as low you can and back the opposing player away from the goal. The spin-off can be performed with either foot.

Tap Move

The tap move is a technique used to fake out an opposing player when rebounding. This technique uses misdirection to catch the opposing player off-guard. To perform the tap move, simply tap the opposing player on either side of his/her body. This should cause the player to shift in that direction and allowing you to go around the opposite side. When you get the inside position, get low and box out.

Rebounding Tips

Here are a few tips that you can use to improve your rebounding ability:

Make Contact

Make contact with the opposing player before you try to grab the rebound. Making the initial contact will knock that player off-balance and make it easier for you to secure the rebound. When a field goal is attempted, hit the opposing player with your forearm or lower body. Get the inside position and use your lower body to maintain contact. Back the player away from the goal then attempt to get the rebound. Making the initial contact is an effective way to catch opposing players off guard. It will be very difficult for them to get back around you as long as you maintain contact.

Stay Low

Stay low while boxing out for a rebound. This will make it difficult for the opposing players to get around you. The lower you are, the lower your center of gravity. The opposing players will struggle to move you out of the way and gain position. Just make sure your maintain contact so they can't slip past you. Each time you box out, be sure to get low and box out strong.

Go Get the Rebound

You will be able to secure more rebounds if you go get the ball as opposed to waiting for it to come to you. Most players box out, but many will only go after the rebounds that come near them. Great rebounders attempt to rebound, no matter where the ball goes. Going after every rebound in this manner takes a lot of effort and effort is the key to rebounding.

Understanding Trajectories

Knowing where the ball will go after a missed shot will greatly increase your chances of securing the rebound. For example, if a shot is missed from the corner, there is a 70% chance that the ball will go to the opposite side. Also, 90% of all rebounds occur below the goal. This percentage indicates that the best place to rebound the ball is around the basket. However, you shouldn't stand directly underneath the goal when you're trying to rebound. Ideally, you'll want to box out at least one to two feet in front of the goal. This will help you to get in the right position to get the rebound.

Keep Your Hands Up

Keep your hands up while boxing out. Doing so will prepare you to quickly reach up and grab a rebound. Bend your arms at a 90-degree angle so that your elbows are out and your hands are up. It will be much harder to secure a rebound if your hands are down by your sides.

Put Forth the Effort

Rebounding isn't about athleticism or brute strength; it's about effort and desire. Usually, the person that gets the rebound is the one that wants it the most. Believe that you can get every rebound and put forth the effort to rebound effectively, especially on defense.

Chin the Ball

Opposing players will often attempt to steal the ball by tipping it away. You can counter this by chinning the ball immediately after you grab the rebound. You'll be holding the ball tighter and sticking out your elbows. This will make it much more difficult for an opposing player to steal the ball from you. If you fail to chin the ball, you'll be giving the opposing team an opportunity to steal it. Steals will lead to turnovers and turnovers will have a negative impact on your team.

Time the Ball

Time the ball when it comes off the rim after a missed shot. Jumping too soon or too late may cause you to miss the opportunity to get the rebound. Wait until the ball is coming down and jump into the air to meet it. Good timing will come with practice. The more you practice your rebounding ability, the better your timing will become.

Box Out the Shooter

Failing to box out the shooter is a costly mistake. It could result in a second chance opportunity for the opposing team. If the shooter is not boxed out, then he/she will have an open path to retrieve the rebound. This is very important to remember, especially when the opposing team is shooting free throws. The player defending the shooter must box out to make sure that he/she doesn't get an offensive rebound.

Shuffle Your Feet

Shuffle your feet when boxing out to keep the opposing player from getting around you. He/she will make every attempt to reclaim the inside position, but it is important that you maintain contact. Feel the opposing player with your lower body and shuffle your feet to maintain contact. Remember to keep your body between your opponent and the basketball.

What is Rebounding All About?

Rebounding is all about position, timing, desire, and effort. Players have to want the rebound more than the opposing team and put forth the effort to secure it. They have to get good position near the goal without being too close or too far away from it. They must box out the opposing player each time a shot is attempted. And, they also need to time their jumps to grab the rebound as it's coming down off the rim.

Rebounding is one of the most important aspects of basketball and it shouldn't be overlooked or underestimated. The team that grabs the most rebounds will have a clear advantage over the other team. Rebounds can be the difference between winning and losing.

Chapter 10 | Defense

"Everything negative – pressure, challenges -- are all an opportunity for me to rise."

– Kobe Bryant

What is Defense?

Defense is the act of preventing the opposing team from scoring. There are several defensive strategies and sets that can be used to defend the offensive team. Individual defenders can hedge, take charges, and use the defensive stance to stop their opponents from scoring the ball.

Poor defensive players will be a liability for the defense. Their poor defensive skills will make their team vulnerable to offensive plays, especially during a man-to-man defense. However, individual players can improve their defensive ability through practice. This will allow them to correct the weaknesses in their defensive capabilities, and become better defenders.

Defense is widely considered to be the most important aspect of basketball. It is a deciding factor for a team's success. The famous quote, "Offense sells tickets, but defense wins games," is true. Teams must play solid defense to prevent the opposing team from scoring the ball.

This chapter will cover a few defensive techniques that players can use to improve their overall defensive ability. Defense isn't as glamorous as offense, but it is no less important. In fact, defense ability is one of the key traits that coaches often look for in a player.

Defensive Techniques
Defensive Stance

Defenders must get into a defensive stance to contain the offensive players on defense. This stance will allow them to quickly cut off a drive, contest a shot, or take a charge. It also allows players to shuffle their feet and move laterally to cut off an offensive player's advancement.

To get into the defensive stance, stand with your feet slightly wider than shoulder width apart (your feet should be pointing outward slightly). Squat down without letting your knees go past your toes. Keep your head up and extend your arms out. You may also keep one arm high and the other low to make it more difficult for the ball-handler to shoot.

You will move by shuffling your feet laterally. Extend one foot out to the left (or right) and then the other. Both feet should be moving in the same direction. But, you must be sure not to cross your feet while you shuffle. Doing so may cause you to lose your balance and fall. Also, try to stay low and on the balls of your feet to maximize your quickness. Trying to defend while flat-footed and/or standing up too high will limit your ability to move quickly around the court.

Defenders will need to use the defensive stance to force the ball-handler to move in a particular direction. They must angle their bodies in way that allows them to cut off the ball-handler. If a defender wants the ball-handler to go left, then he/she will defend on the right side and vice-versa. The defender can keep cutting off the ball-handler in this manner until he/she picks up the ball. This may both frustrate and tire the ball-handler out. Frustration and fatigue will likely cause the offensive team to make mistakes that the defense can capitalize on.

There may be times when a defender is unable to cut off the ball-handler's advancement in the open court. In this situation, the defender can get out of the defensive stance and run to keep up with the ball-handler. For example, if the ball-handler passes the defender, that defender may have to turn and run to catch up. The defender should be able to catch up depending on how far the ball-handler is from the goal.

Close Out

When defenders approach the ball-handler on the perimeter, they should close out. Closing out allows the defender to quickly contest a shot attempt or get into position to defend a drive. To close out, sprint toward the player with the ball. When you are a few feet away, start to chop your feet and put your hands in the air. When you reach the ball-handler, get into a defensive stance and play defense as usual.

There are several mistakes that can be made when attempting a close out. Any one of them may allow the ball-handler to get an open shot at the goal. The first mistake is that players may try sprint straight toward the ball-handler without chopping their feet. This can result in the offensive player dribbling right past them and heading toward the goal. Chopping your feet will allow you slow down so that you can defend. Another common mistake is jump or lunge at the ball-handler. This is usually done in an effort to block a shot attempt. However, good offensive players will pump fake and go right past the defender. Staying on the ground and closing out will allow the defender to quickly cut off a drive. They will also be able to jump and contest the jump shot from this position if they need to. The close out should be used in situations in which the defender must run to meet an offensive player on the perimeter. For example, the ball gets passed to an open player on the wing and the defender must hurry to defend him/her.

Get in the Passing Lanes

In a man-to-man defense, defenders that are one pass away from the ball should get into the passing lane. The passing lane is the path between two offensive players (one player being the ball-handler). This invisible path is the trajectory that the ball would have to travel if the ball-handler passes it to a teammate. When a defender is one pass away, he/she should get a hand in the passing lane to deny the pass.

Defenders must be careful when they are denying a pass. The offensive players that they are guarding could attempt to cut the goal. Crafty offensive players will often try to use the opportunity to get to the ball and score. The defense should be prepared for this situation and be able to stop it when it happens.

Denying the pass is a common defensive technique that many high-level basketball teams use. It forces the ball-handler to work that much harder to get the ball to a teammate. Meanwhile, the defensive player guarding the ball-handler can pressure and try to force a five-second violation. Players that aren't one pass away should move toward the ball in case they need to help out.

Help-Side Defense

Help-side defense occurs when a defender is more than one pass away from the ball. That defender will shift to help a teammate defend the ball-handler. Many teams use help defense to effectively contain the offense. When the ball is on one side of the court, the defenders that are more than one pass away will move toward the ball-handler. These players won't closely defend their defensive assignments unless specified by a coach. Help-side defense can be very effective at stopping the offense, but the defense must make good rotations.

Playing a Zone Defense

In a zone defense, each defender will have an area to defend. They will have to guard any player that steps into their designated area. The boundaries for these areas depend on the defensive set that is currently being used by the defense. Zone defenses are effective against teams that like to drive to the goal, set screens, or make back door cuts. Zone defenses are weak against teams that have good three-point shooters. Zones can also be exploited if the offensive team is able to take advantage of the gaps in the defense (the space between each defender). Offensive players can attempt to use these gaps to get to the basket and score. A zone can also, in some ways, make up for weak defenders.

Dealing with screens

Call Out the Screen

Defenders must call out every screen that's set by their defensive assignment. The defenders must notify their teammates that a screen is about to be set. They must also tell their teammate which side the screen is coming from. This should give the defender (that is being screened) enough time to maneuver around the screen and keep from running into it. The defensive player only needs to yell "screen" and the direction that the screen is coming from before it is set (ex. screen right, screen left). Failing to communicate with your teammates may cause them to get screened, and an offensive player to get open. Calling out screens will limit their effectiveness.

Hedge the Screen

Hedging is a great defensive technique that is used to defend ball screens. When a screen is set, the defender that's guarding the screener can hedge the screen to slow down the ball-handler. To hedge a screen, the defender will step up and block the path of the ball-handler. This will force the ball-handler to dribble around the hedger and give the defender enough time recover. After the defender recovers, the hedger will return to his/her previous defensive assignment.

To counter the hedge, the offense may attempt to slip to the goal. Alternatively, the ball-handler may wait until the hedger returns to his/her matchup and then shoot a jump shot before the other defender can recover.

Opening Up on the Screen

When a screen is set, the defender that is guarding the screener must open up and let his/her teammate get through. Opening up on the screen will give the screened player the room to maneuver around it. To open up on a screen, the defender will back one to two feet away from the player setting the screen. As soon as the other defender gets through, the player (that opened up) will recover to his/her defensive assignment.

Going Under the Screen

Players can quickly get around a screen by going underneath it. When a screen is set, the defender being screened can go around the screener and continue to defend the ball-handler. However, this can only happen if the defender guarding the screener opens up and lets the defender get through. Going under the screen does have a disadvantage. It can give the ball-handler an opportunity to take a quick shot while the defender is trying to recover. However, the defender can hedge the screen to limit this problem.

Going Over the Top of the Screen

When a defender goes over the top of a screen, he/she will squeeze in-between the ball-handler and the screener. The defender must take a big step to get between both players and continue guarding the ball-handler. The screen may hit the defender a bit, but he/she should be able to recover in time.

Trailing an Offensive Player

Another option when dealing with screens is to trail the offensive player. Typically, this option is only for screens set off the ball. When an offensive player uses a screen, the defender can follow right behind that player. Defenders must follow closely behind the offensive players, or they may lose them. If the offensive player receives the ball, the defender should be right there to defend. This is a great technique for dealing with off the ball screens. It is one that's used by many defenders.

Switching on the Screen

Occasionally, defenders will switch defensive assignments when a screen is set. Switching matchups in this manner will nullify the screen's effectiveness. It allows the defenders to continue defending without forcing them to get through the screen. When an offensive player sets a screen, the two defenders involved will swap defensive assignments. Switching can be a great defensive strategy in a man-to-man defense, but it can also put the defense at a disadvantage. Switching can lead to match-up problems because any offensive player (except the ball-handler) can set a screen for another teammate. For example, the point guard could end up guarding the center or vice versa. This could lead to a mismatched situation and an easy scoring opportunity for the offense.

Keys to Good Team Defense

Awareness

Take notice of where the offensive players are located on the court. Notice their movements and make sure that no one is left unguarded. You can do this by being aware of their surroundings on defense. Being aware off the offensive players' location will help to limit open jump shots, cuts to the paint, and players trying to sneak through gaps in the defense.

Communication

For any defensive set to be effective, the defense must communicate. The defensive team must call out all screens, open player locations, and other offensive movements. Communication is vital to a team's success.

Anticipation

Teams must anticipate an offensive play by noticing where the ball will be passed, or when a shot is about to be taken. They should be ready to take action at all times. The defense needs to be able to quickly move to a spot or get in the passing lane to tip away a pass.

Chapter 11 | Defensive Sets

"Love never fails. Character never quits. And with patience and persistence, dreams do come true."
– Pete Maravich

A team can run several different defensive sets during a game. Each set is uses a different strategy to stop the offensive team from scoring. This chapter covers some of the most popular defensive sets along with their strengths and weaknesses.

1-2-2

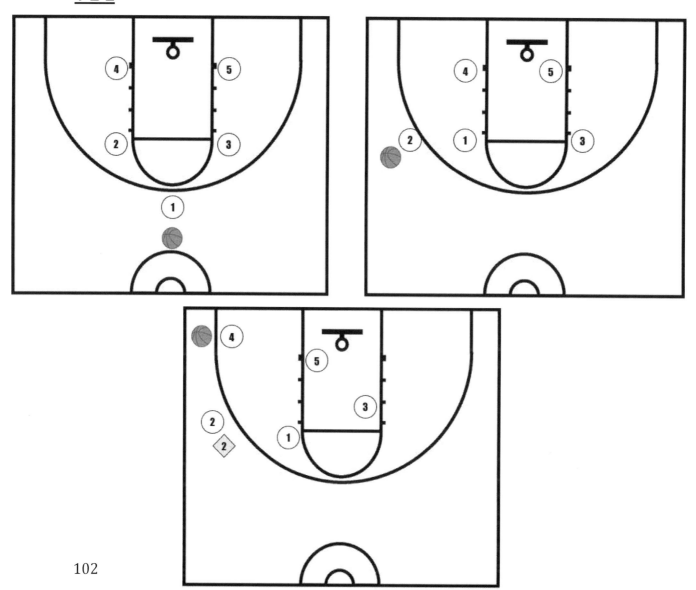

The 1-2-2 is a zone defense that is often used to counter outside shooting teams. The point guard will be positioned at the top of the defense, the shooting guard and small forward will be at the corners of the free throw line, and a post player will be on each block. For this defense to be effective, the defensive players must know their rotations. They must be able to rotate quickly when the ball is passed or when a defender goes to trap. If the players fail to rotate, then there will be gaps in the defense that the offensive team can exploit.

The 1-2-2 is effective against good outside shooting teams. It allows the defense to trap in certain areas and put pressure on the offensive players on the perimeter.

1-2-2 Strengths:

Pressures Players on the Perimeter

This defense can put a lot of pressure on the ball-handler. No matter where he/she goes, there will be a defender to apply defensive pressure. Defenders may even cut off the passing lanes so it will be difficult for the ball-handler to get the ball to a teammate.

Ability to Trap

There are certain areas of the court in which the defense may trap the ball-handler. This can put even more pressure on the offense and lead to a turnover, which can in turn become a fast break opportunity.

Pressures Three-Point Shooters

Because the 1-2-2 puts pressure on the perimeter players, it becomes more difficult for the offense to shoot three-pointers. When an offensive player attempts a three-pointer, a defender will usually be in position to contest it.

1-2-2 Weaknesses:

The High Post Area

In the 1-2-2, there is a gap in-between the defender in the post and the defender at the high post. An offensive player could slip between these two players, receive the ball, and score. However, the defense can use communication and good rotations to minimize this vulnerability.

Corner of the Three-point Line

The corner can also be a vulnerable spot for this defense. An offensive player may be able to attack the zone or shoot an open three from the corner. Once again, good rotations and communication can help to limit this weakness.

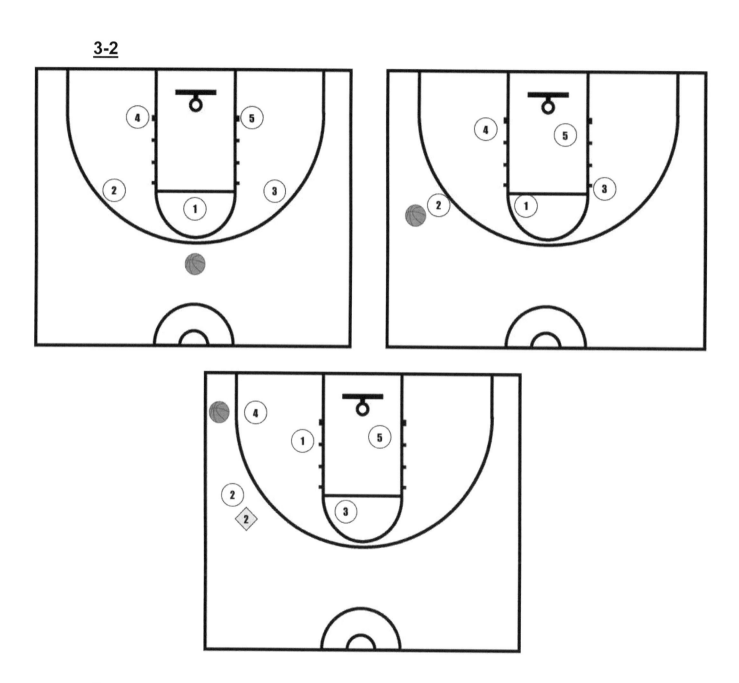

3-2

The 3-2 zone is very similar to the 1-2-2. Three defenders are positioned at the top of the zone (around the free throw line) and two are positioned at the bottom (around the post). One guard (usually the point guard) will be at the free throw line and two players will be at each of the free throw line extended areas. There will also be one post player positioned on each block. This is same formation as the 1-2-2 zone except that the point guard (or whoever the top defender is) will be at the free throw line and the other top players will be spread further out. Since the two zones are so similar, they share many of the same strengths and weaknesses. However, there are still a few subtle differences.

3-2 Strengths:

The High Post Area

In the 1-2-2, the high post is a vulnerable area. But, the 3-2 corrects this weakness due to its formation. Because the point guard stays around the high post area, it is much more difficult for the offense to take advantage.

3-2 Weaknesses:

Three-point Shooting

If the offensive point guard can shoot three-pointers, then it may cause a problem. That point guard could shoot wide open three-pointer while the defender is at the high post.

<u>2-3</u>

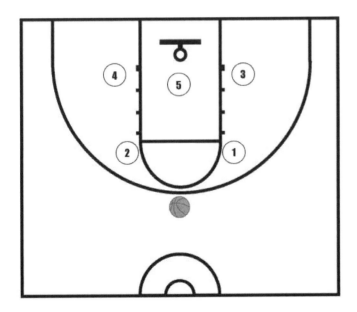
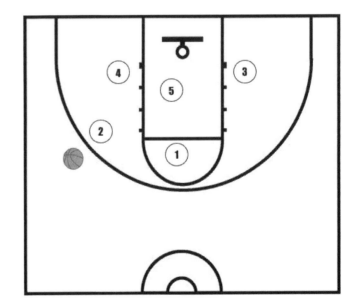

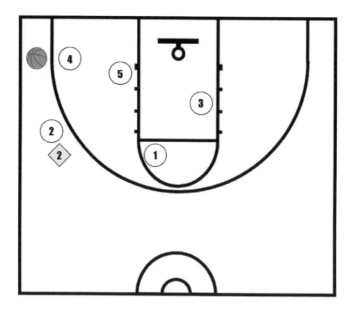

The 2-3 zone is the most common zone defense one of the most widely used defenses in basketball. Teams usually alternate between this defensive set and the man-to-man defense. The formation of the 2-3 zone is exactly as the name suggests. One guard will be positioned at each corner of the free throw line, one forward will be on each block (or short corner), and the center will be in the middle of the paint.

This zone, like many others, is reactive. The defense reacts to the offense's movements and acts accordingly. This zone relies on great defensive rotations to be effective. Each defender defends an invisible area on the court. If an offensive player enters that zone, then the defender will begin to defend that player. This is where the rotations come into play. When that defender moves to guard the offensive player, the rest of the defenders will shift. It should be as though all the defenders on the court are attached to each other with an invisible thread. When one defender moves, so will another. Typically, the defenders will move in the direction of the ball.

There may be a situation when there is an unguarded offensive player on the opposite side from the ball. This player would have been left open when all the defenders shifted toward the ball. This situation is acceptable because ball-handler would have to make a lob pass to get the ball to that player. The defense should have ample time to adjust and be ready to defend when the ball is received. Communication is very important in this situation because the defense needs to be aware of the open players on the court.

The 2-3 zone is great for defending the paint. The defense makes it difficult for the offense to score near the basket. It is also works well against teams that like to penetrate and cut to the basket. The zone is also an effective deterrent against screens, both on and off the ball. The defenders' rotations and positioning make it hard for the offense to capitalize on a screen.

Because the 2-3 zone is so good at defending the paint, it is very good at stopping the opposing team from scoring in the post. Post players score most of their points in the paint so the zone is a great way to hinder their scoring ability. Post players may have to change their strategy or move to another area to score the ball. Good post players could still find a way to score, but it won't be easy to score down low.

Teams that are bad defensively tend to use the 2-3 zone. It helps to mask the fact that they don't play very good defense. Since the defenders guard zones and not certain players, the 2-3 zone can make up for poor one-on-one defenders. For example, if the offensive players keep getting to the basket, the defense can get into the 2-3. The defense can stop the offense from getting into the paint and force them to shoot an outside shot.

The overall effectiveness of this defense will depend on communication and teamwork.

2-3 Strengths:

Forcing the Outside Shot

The 2-3 zone defense is great for forcing the offense to shoot outside shots. For obvious reasons, outside shots are more difficult to make than those taken near the basket. So forcing a team to shoot a three-pointer can create an advantage for the defense. This is especially true against poor outside shooting teams. However, forcing outside shots can also be a weakness of this zone.

Stopping Dribble Penetration

The 2-3 zone is also great for cutting off drives to the basket. There should always be a defender waiting to cut the ball-handler off before he/she can make it to the goal.

Defending the Paint

Because of the formation of the defense, it is very effective at defending the paint. Guards and post players alike should have a difficult time scoring in the paint because of the defensive pressure in the lane.

Hiding Bad Defenders

The 2-3 zone can hide bad defensive players because they will only have to defend an area and not a specific player. The zone also lowers the chance that an offensive player could or would drive to the lane. Also, defenders shouldn't have to worry about screens, though there are a few offensive plays that incorporate screens against this zone. Poor defenders will simply have to do their best to guard their area. Their teammates will act as a safety net in case they get into trouble.

Slowing Down the Offense

The zone can be useful for slowing down the offense. The offense may have a tougher time scoring against the zone than they would against a man-to-man defense. They will likely have to swing the ball several times to even get a decent shot opportunity. There are only a few offensive plays that can be run to counter a zone defense. The offense may end up wasting a possession if they are unable to get a good field goal opportunity.

2-3 Weaknesses:

3-point Shooting

The 2-3 zone is a great way to force the offense to take outside shots. But what if the offensive team excels at outside shooting? Then one of the 2-3's strengths will become a weakness. If a team is consistently making their three-point shots, then the defense must adjust and try a different set.

Playing From Behind

Because this defense slows down the game, it makes it difficult for a team to comeback from a deficit. This is especially true if the team is losing in the fourth quarter with time is running out. In this situation, a man-to-man defense would be more appropriate.

Gaps in the Zone

There are gaps in the zone between the defenders. The offense may be able to take advantage of these gaps. If an offensive player is allowed to get behind the defense unnoticed, then that player may be able to get the ball and score. This is another situation in which communication is very important. The defense needs to be aware of the offensive players.

Creates an Unbalanced Floor

The 2-3 zone can create an unbalanced floor for the defense. For example, there can be four defenders on one side of the court and only one on the other. If the offense attempts to take advantage of this situation, the defense should be able to adjust. However, it could still be considered a weakness if the defense is unable to make the adjustments and rotate in time. This is why good rotations and communication are so important in the 2-3 zone.

Man-to-man

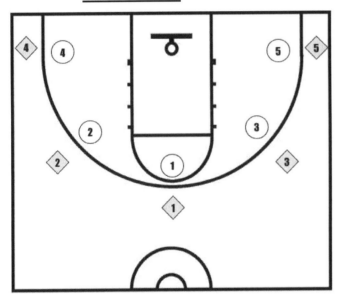

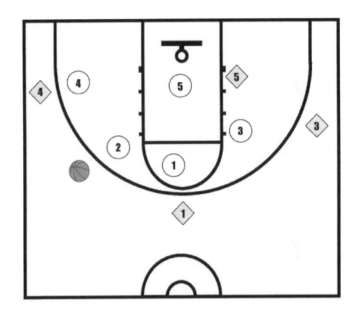

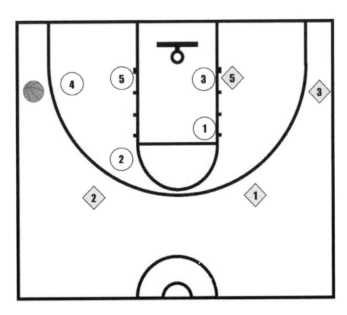

The man-to-man defense is the most common defense in basketball. Unlike a zone defense, each defender will have to defend at least one offensive player. Most of the time, this offensive player will be at the same position as the defender. However, it is not uncommon for players of different positions to guard each other. For example, the power forward could guard the small forward or vice versa.

The man-to-man is flexible in what it allows the defenders to do. Players are not forced to defend the same player for the duration of the game or even for the duration of a single play. Defenders can switch at any time as long as they are not guarding the ball-handler. For example, the point guard could switch on a screen at end up defending the opposing team's small forward. Another scenario is when the coach calls for two players to switch defensive assignments during a play. Defenders may also double-team the ball-handler. For example, a defender may leave his/her defensive assignment to double team the ball-handler with a teammate. Effective double teams can put pressure on the offense and lead to turnovers.

Man-to-Man Strengths:

Aggression

The man-to-man is a more aggressive defense than the zone. It allows the defenders to really put pressure on their defensive assignment for the duration of a play. Since the defenders are only assigned to one offensive player, they can focus on stopping that player from scoring the ball.

Easier to Play from Behind

The man-to-man is the defense that team's should use when they're losing. This defense will speed up the tempo of the game. Increased pressure on the offense will make it difficult for them to hold the ball for extended periods of time. The defense can attempt to force mistakes and turnovers which can turn into scoring opportunities. These opportunities can allow a team to make up the deficit or even take the lead. Teams will often switch to a man-to-man defense when they fall behind, especially in the fourth quarter.

Defending Strong Offensive Players

In a man-to-man defense, the opposing team's best offensive player will always be guarded by at least one defender. In a zone, that player may not always be directly defended. In the man-to-man, just one defender or two with a double team will pressure the player.

Man-to-Man Weaknesses:

Screens are More Effective

In a zone, screens become relatively ineffective because the defenders are just guarding areas. However, the opposite is true for the man-to-man defense. In this defense, offensive players can use screens to great effect to get open shots. The screens will block the defenders' path and hinder them from defending the offensive players. Offensive plays often involve the use of screens to get players open. To counteract these screens, defenders must use one of the techniques for dealing with screens.

Exposes Bad Defenders

Unlike the 2-3 zone, this defense doesn't make up for a defender's lack of defensive ability. In a zone, the rotations and the fact that players defend areas make up for shortcomings of a bad defender. In a man-to-man, defenders must guard players on their own (with a few exceptions). Defenders will have to use their individual defensive ability to guard the opposing players. If a defender doesn't have solid defensive ability, then it will be easier for the offensive player to score.

Makes it Difficult to Help

When the offensive player gets past a defender, another defender will usually help. However, the man-to-man defense makes this a bit more difficult to pull off. Helping a defender in this manner would mean leaving another player unguarded. Leaving offensive players open could lead to scoring opportunities. Defenders can make use of quick rotations to minimize this weakness.

Full-Court Press

The full-court press is a common defensive strategy that involves pressuring the offensive team for the entire length of the court. The pressure applied to the offense is similar to that of a half-court defensive set. The full-court press is an aggressive defense that involves two different types: man-to-man and zone. The distinction between the two types is the same as the half-court sets.

Full-Court Press (Zone):

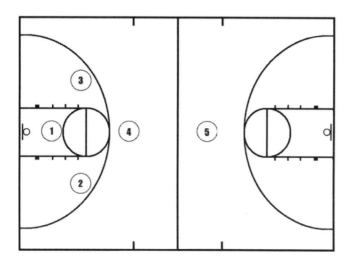
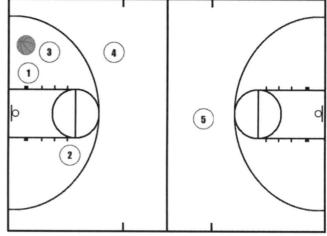

Full-Court Press (Man-to-Man):

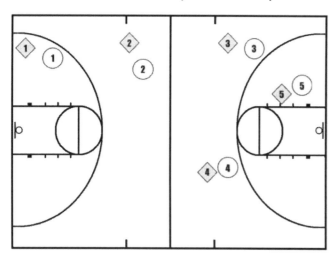
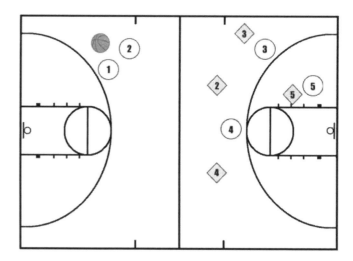

Full-court presses take a tremendous amount of effort from the defense, but they can also be very effective against an offense. Usually, a defender will pressure the inbound pass and make it difficult for the offense to get the ball inbounded. The defense is attempting to cause a five-second violation, make the offensive player catch the ball in a bad position, or just make things more difficult for the offense. If the ball is successfully inbounded, then the defenders may attempt to trap the ball-handler in the backcourt or around the half-court line.

If performed correctly, the full-court press can take its toll and tire out the offense. However, it could tire out the defense as well. The full-court press can be used to force turnovers and make it difficult for the offense to bring the ball up the court.

Full-Court Press Strengths:

Takes Advantage of the Offense's Weaknesses

This press can take advantage of the offensive team's shortcomings. Ineffective ball-handlers, weak passers, and slow offenses can all turn into opportunities for the defense. The full-court press can put the offense in a bad situation if they have some of these problems. For example, the full-court pressure can cause the ball to be stolen from the ball-handler, a pass to get intercepted, or a slow offense to struggle.

Tires Out the Offense

As discussed before, the press can tire out the offense. If the press is used consistently, then the offense will continuously have to break it, which can be extremely tiring.

Forces Turnovers

The full-court press can be used to force turnovers. It can cause the offensive players to get tired and frustrated, which may lead to mistakes and turnovers.

Full-Court Press Weaknesses:

Press Breaks

The defense can be left at a huge disadvantage if the press is broken. Press breaks can leave the defense vulnerable to fast breaks and open jump shots. The defense will have to quickly recover if the press is broken by the offense.

Tires Out Defenders

Just as the press can tire out offensive players, it can also tire out the defense. Presses take a lot of energy and effort to perform so the defense could easily tire out if they're not well conditioned.

Half-Court Press

The half-court press is just like the full-court version, except that it occurs after the ball crosses half-court. However, it's not always the same. It will depend on the type of half-court press that's being run. This press shares nearly all of the strengths of the full-court press though it eliminates some its weaknesses. For example, it may not tire out the defenders as much and press breaks may be less effective in a half-court setting.

Chapter 12 | Steals

"I'm a competitive person. I love the game of basketball I'm a gym rat."
–Paul Pierce

What's a Steal?

Steals occur when a defender is able to take the ball from the ball-handler. The defender can steal the ball by intercepting a pass or taking the ball from the ball-handler. Defenders can also tip the ball to a teammate and still get credit for the steal. If the defender touches the offensive player's hands or arms while attempting a steal, then a foul will be called. If the referee calls a foul, then the defender will not get credit for the steal, regardless of whether the ball was actually stolen. Committing a foul when attempting a steal will benefit the offensive team, especially if that team is in the bonus.

Who Gets the Credit?

If the defender tips the ball away from the ball-handler but fails to gain possession of the ball, then a steal will not be credited. A steal will also not be credited if the offensive player accidentally passes the ball straight to a defender. When the ball-handler loses the ball, he/she will be awarded a turnover. The defense is always trying to force turnovers and steals are one of the most common types of turnovers.

Abilities for Stealing the Basketball

It takes a bit of skill to be able to steal the ball from an offensive player, especially if that player is a good ball-handler. To be considered a thief on defense, several skills may be necessary, such as anticipation, reflexes, and quickness.

Defenders need to anticipate where the ball will be or where it is going. This is important for intercepting passes. Defenders do this by using a combination of experience and the ability to pick up on cues from the ball-handler. For example, the ball-handler may look at or move toward the intended recipient of a pass. The defender will notice this and anticipate a pass to that player. At this point other abilities begin come into play to intercept the pass and get the steal. Anticipation is also used to steal the ball while the ball-handler is dribbling. A good defender will be able to anticipate when to reach (and when not to reach) in to tip the ball away from the ball-handler. The defender must identify the type of move that is about to be made or simply judge the height of the ball. Again, this is the point at which the other abilities come into play.

The next ability is the use of reflexes. Reflexes are needed to react in time to intercept a pass or tip the ball away. Webster's dictionary defines reflexes as, "the process that culminates in a reflex and comprises reception, transmission, and reaction," or, "the power of action or responding with adequate speed." So basically, a defender will see an opportunity for a steal, the brain will process what is being seen, and the body will react. Some people possess naturally quick reflexes, but reflexes can also be developed for improvement. A few ways to improve your reflexes are to play catch with any type of ball (like a tennis ball) or simply play basketball and gain more experience. Reflexes are useful in many aspects of basketball like catching the ball, reacting to changes in the defense, or using an offensive move. Players of any sport will benefit from increased reflexes and basketball is no exception. You should take the time to develop them if you want to gain a bit of an edge on the competition.

Defenders must also be quick enough to get their hand in the right place to actually get the steal. Good ball-handlers will move the ball very quickly (both when passing and dribbling), so it's important for players to move their hands quickly to tip it away. Hand quickness can be developed through weight training and practice.

What Not to Do

Do not gamble on steals. Try not to attempt a steal in a way that could take you out of the play. Coaches really try to stress the idea that players should play it safe when trying to steal the ball. For the most part, they would prefer that their team play solid defense rather than make risky defensive plays. When players take themselves out of a play because of a failed steal attempt, it puts the defense at a disadvantage. There will only be four players available to maintain defensive pressure until that player can recover. This can lead to easy points for the offense. It would be in the team's best interest to avoid a 4-on-5 situation. However, this doesn't mean that you should never attempt a steal. My recommendation is that you use your best judgment. Don't lunge at the ball-handler or try to intercept every pass that the offense makes. Just look for the right opportunity and quickly assess the situation. Steals can have a great impact for both teams. The opposing team will be awarded a turnover and your team has an offensive opportunity. It can even lead to easy points on offense if the steal leads to a fast break. Not all steals will lead to fast breaks, but the ones that do can be a great opportunity for your team.

Who Can Steal the Ball?

There is no designated player that is expected to steal the ball. Any position can attempt to make a steal while on defense. However, not every player is encouraged to do so. With that said, smaller guards usually get the majority of the steals for their team. This is because they are often guarding the player that is in possession of the basketball, such the point guard or shooting guard. These guards are usually very quick and physically more capable of stealing the ball.

Chapter 13 | Blocks

"Every time you compete,
try harder to improve on
your last performance."
– *Elgin Baylor*

What's a Block?

A block occurs when a defensive player deflects an offensive player's shot after it is released. The ball must not be traveling downward toward the rim when the defender deflects the ball, or a goaltending violation will be called. A goaltending violation will also be called if the ball is touched after it bounces off the backboard. To be considered legal, a shot must be blocked no later than at its apex. Defenders must also be careful not to touch the shooter's hand or body while attempting to block a shot. Making contact with the shooter will result in a foul and free throws for the offensive player. If a foul is committed, the block will not be counted even if the defender that blocked the shot and defender that committed the foul are different players. Blocked shots are recorded as missed field goals. A blocked shot that still makes it into the basket is recorded as a successful field goal and the block is not counted.

Do Size and Position Play a Part in Shot Blocking?

A player's height and position play an important part in shot blocking. Often, the tallest players will record most of the blocks for their team. The greatest shot blockers throughout history have been well over 6 feet and some were as tall as 7 feet. Players with exceptional height typically have the advantage when attempting to block the shots of shorter players.

The position of the player is also important because some players, such as the power forward and center, are positioned around the basket on offense and defense. Players at these positions are in the perfect location to block shots, especially against offensive players that drive to the goal.

Although height and position are important, they're not the most important characteristics of a great shot blocker. There are certain abilities that can be developed to increase a player's shot blocking capabilities.

Abilities for Shot Blocking

The abilities of a successful shot blocker include anticipation, hand-eye coordination, timing, and athleticism. Defenders must be able to anticipate the shot to have a chance at blocking it. Hand-eye coordination is necessary for a defender to see the ball and move his or her hand to deflect it in time. Timing (which is the most important ability for shot blocking) allows players to jump at the right time to block the shot. If a defender jumps too early, the offensive player will be rising as the defender is coming down. If the defender jumps too late, the offensive player will release the ball before the defender can block it. Both situations can easily lead to a defensive foul. Athleticism is the least important of the abilities, but it can still make a big difference. Defensive players with good athletic ability will have a larger window of opportunity to block a shot. They can rise up and meet the ball in the air to block it as opposed to blocking the shot as soon as it is released from the shooter's hands.

Benefits of Shot Blocking

Shot blocking can have a demoralizing effect on the offense. If a defender is a known shot blocker or blocks several shots during a game, then the offense may shy away from that player. They may hesitate to drive to the basket or attempt to shoot over that defender. This could lead to missed shots and scoring opportunities for the offense. Shot blocking can intimidate offensive players and lead to a huge advantage for the defensive team.

Chapter 14 | Basketball Drills

"I can accept failure, everyone fails at something. But I can't accept not trying."

– *Michael Jordan*

Shooting Drills

This section features several drills that can allow players to improve their shooting ability. One player, along with an optional rebounder/passer, can perform nearly all the drills in this section. When performing the shooting drills, be sure to only count the shots that you make and not those that you miss.

Form Shooting:

Form shooting can help players improve their shooting form. The repetition of the drill will allow them to perfect their form over time. To perform the drill, stand about one foot in front of the goal with the basketball. Your body should be facing the basket. Slowly shoot the ball while focusing specifically on your form. You will only be using your upper body during this drill; therefore there will be no need to bend your knees before you release the ball. Keep both feet on the ground and your eyes on the goal. Perform a set of form shots from one spot, then take a step back and perform another set of shots. Keep shooting and stepping back until you have reached the free throw line. Complete the drill by shooting free throws. You can perform this drill from various angles, but the center of the paint (in front of the goal) is the default starting position.

Perform no less than 50 form shots, 10 at each spot.

Elbow-to-Elbow Shooting Drill:

The elbow-to-elbow is a drill in which a player will shoot from both corners of the free throw line. The drill conditions players to run to quickly catch the ball and shoot. This drill can be performed with one or more people. Another player could be the rebounder and/or passer. The following description assumes that there is a second person assisting with the drill. To perform the drill, start at one of the corners (of the free throw line) with the ball. Get into a shooting stance and await the pass. As soon as you receive the ball, perform a jump shot. After the ball is released, run to the opposite elbow and repeat the process. Keep alternating elbows for the duration of the drill. If you are the one performing the drill, then you will toss the ball to yourself and get your own rebounds.

Perform no less than 20 shots, 10 on each elbow.

15-Foot Jumpers Off the Backboard:

This drill improves will improve a player's ability to make shots using the backboard. To perform the drill, start around the free-throw line extended area (between the three-point line and the block). Get into a shooting stance and prepare to receive the pass. As soon as the ball is received, shoot the ball off the backboard. Be sure to aim for the top corner of the square. After the ball is released, run to the same spot on the opposite side of the goal and repeat.

Perform no less than 20 shots, 10 on each side.

Short Corner Jumpers:

This drill is similar to the previous two drills, except that the shots will be taken from the short corner. To perform the drill, start at the short corner with the ball. Get into the shooting stance and await the pass. When you receive the ball, shoot a jump shot. As soon as the ball is released, sprint to the opposite short corner and get ready to take another shot. Keep alternating between the two short corners for the duration of the drill.

Perform no less that 20 shots, 10 at each short corner.

10 Jumpers, 10 Layups Drill:

The 10 jumpers, 10 layups is a drill that improves both conditioning and shooting ability. The drill forces players to stay focused while they're fatigued. To perform the drill, start at half court with the basketball and face either goal. Dribble toward the basket and perform a layup. Get the rebound and dribble down the court toward the opposite goal. Stop around the free throw line and perform a pull-up jumper. Get your rebound and dribble back down the court toward the opposite goal. Repeat until you have shot at total of 10 jumpers and 10 layups. This drill should be performed as quickly as possible. You can even add a time limit to make things more difficult. If you are performing this drill with a partner, then one person will be the rebound the jump shots. You may get fatigued during the drill, but try to maintain your focus.

Perform this drill no less than 2 times.

Catch & Shooting on the Move Drill:

This drill improves the player's ability to catch the ball and shoot a quick jump shot in transition. To perform the drill, start at the three-point or free throw line. Another player will need to stand underneath the goal to be the rebounder and the passer. Get into a shooting stance and await the pass. The player under the goal will pass the ball to start the drill. As soon as you receive the ball, perform a jump shot. After the ball is released, backpedal to half court and sprint back to the starting position. The other player will rebound the ball and pass it back to you. Repeat this process until the drill is complete. You may also get your own rebounds if you don't have another player rebounding for you.

Perform no less than 10 shots.

Spot Shooting:

In this drill, players will shoot the ball from five different spots: both short corners, both free throw line extended areas, and the free throw line. You will shoot one shot at each of these locations to complete one rotation of the drill. After the first rotation, you will start from the location of your last shot (one of the short corners). To perform the drill, begin at either short corner. There should be a person under the goal acting as the passer and rebounder. Get into a shooting stance and prepare to receive the ball. As soon as you receive the ball, perform a jump shot from the short corner. After the ball is released, run to the next spot and repeat.

You can also perform this drill around the three-point line. The spots will be at the same angles, just behind the three-point line. Perform the drill in the same manner as before.

Perform no less than 20 shots.

One Dribble Pull-up Jumper Drill:

This drill involves the same locations as the spot shooting drill. Another player will stand underneath the goal to rebound and pass. Start at the short corner and await the pass. When you receive the ball, take one dribble and shoot. The transition from the dribble to the shot should be one fluid motion. As soon as the ball is released, run to the next spot and repeat. Try to dribble in a different direction after every few shots.

Perform no less than 20 shots.

Pump Fake, One Dribble, Pull-up Jumper Drill:

These moves are used to get a defender in the air so the ball-handler can get an open shot. There will need to be a person under the goal to rebound and pass the ball. To perform the drill, start at one of the five spots and await the pass. As soon as you receive the ball, perform a pump fake, take one dribble, and shoot a jump shot. After the ball is released, run to the next spot and repeat. Try to change the direction you dribble in after every few shots.

Perform no less than 20 jumpers, 10 on each side.

Shoot, Slide, Run Drill:

This is a shooting and conditioning drill. Players will shoot jump shots, perform defensive slides, and sprint around the court. The drill can improve a player's ability to focus while fatigued. To perform the drill, start at one of the five shooting spots and prepare to receive the ball. As soon you receive the ball, perform a jump shot. After the ball is released, perform a defensive slide to the sideline furthest from you. If you are at the top of the key, slide to the sideline opposite to the one you previously went to. After touching the sideline, sprint back to the starting point and shoot another jump shot.

Perform no less than 5 shots in each spot.

3-Man Shooting Drill:

3-man shooting is a shooting drill that is performed with three people. There will be one shooter, one passer, and one rebounder. Two basketballs can be used to speed up the drill. To perform the drill, the passer and rebounder will begin with one basketball each. The shooter will get into a shooting stance and await the pass. The passer will pass the ball to the shooter for a jump shot. At the same time, the rebounder will get the ball and become the passer. The passer will now become the shooter and the shooter will become the rebounder. Now the process will start over again. Alternatively, the shooter can shoot a specified number of shots before everyone rotates. Each player should get a chance to shoot, pass, and rebound the ball. This drill makes it easier to shoot a lot of shots in a short amount of time.

Perform no less that 30 shots before rotating.

Sweep-Through Drill:

This drill improves the speed and technique of a player's sweep-through move. While this drill can be performed with one player, it is more effective with two. To perform the drill, start on the perimeter (facing away from the goal) with a player defending you. Toss the ball to yourself, turn, and sweep it across your body. Keep the ball low and take a big step past the defender. As soon as you pass the defender, head toward the goal and perform a layup.

Perform no less than 20 swing-through moves, 10 on each side of the court.

Jump Stop Drill:

The jump stop drill can be performed with one or two players, but this description involves two. To perform the drill, start on the wing with the ball. The other player will start in the paint with his/her hands up. Dribble toward the goal and perform a jump stop around that player. As soon as you pass the other player, jump and perform a layup. If only one player is performing the drill, then a chair will take the place of the second player.

Perform no less than 10 jump stops.

Finishing Drill:

The finishing drill improves a player's ability to finish a play after being fouled. It can allow players to become accustomed to taking contact in the paint. Two players are required to perform this drill, one to score the ball and the other to make the foul. The fouling player can also use a blocking pad, which is a safer way to foul the shooter. To perform the drill, start in the paint with the ball. The other player will stand underneath the goal. Take a step toward the goal and perform a layup while the other player makes the foul. Power through the contact and score the ball. The foul should be made across the arms to minimize chance of injury. Any type of move can be used to get to the goal as long as you finish with a layup.

Perform no less than 10 shots in the paint.

Mikan Drill:

The Mikan drill improves coordination and footwork. Post players often use this drill to improve their footwork in the post. To perform the drill, stand under the goal with the ball. Jump (using either foot) and perform a layup with your outside hand. As soon as the ball goes through the net, grab it and perform a layup with the opposite foot and hand. Continue to alternating sides for the duration of the drill. Try to establish a rhythm while performing the drill. Keep your arms up high and don't allow the ball to drop below you chin.

Perform the no less than 20 layups, 10 on each side of the goal.

Passing Drills

Pass to Spot on the Wall:

This drill is used to increase a player's passing accuracy. To perform the drill, stand by a wall with the basketball. Choose an area on the wall to use as a target and aim your pass toward that area. Make a chest, bounce, behind-the-back, or overhead pass and attempt to hit the area on the wall. After a couple of passes, pick a new pass and area on the wall. Practice some of the passes you have learned.

Perform no less than 10 passes.

2-man Passing:

To perform the drill, start with the basketball and have another player stand about 10 feet in front of you. Use any type of pass to get the ball to the other player. That player will catch the ball and pass it back to you using the same type of pass. You and your partner will pass the ball back and forth. After a few passes, you can switch to a different type of pass. After a certain number of passes you and your partner will back farther away from each other to continue the drill.

Perform this for no less than 30 seconds.

2-man Passing and Shuffle (Full Court):

To perform this drill, start on one side of the lane with the basketball. The other player will start on the opposite side of the lane. Start to shuffle down the court at the same time as your partner. Pass the ball to the other player after one or two slides. That player will catch the ball and pass it back to you. Pass the ball back and forth until you both reach the opposite baseline. You both will then perform the drill back to the starting location.

Perform this drill no less than 1 time.

Catching Drills

Catching Drill w/ Tennis Balls:

The catching drill improves a player's ability to catch the ball. If players can catch a small tennis ball then they'll be able to catch a basketball. The drill is often used to help players learn to catch the ball. Two people are required to perform the drill, one person to throw the ball and the other to catch. To perform the drill, place one hand behind your back, get low, and prepare to catch the ball. The other person will stand about 10-15 feet away and throw the tennis ball toward you. Catch it with one hand and throw it back. Perform a set number of catches with one hand then use the opposite hand. To make the drill more difficult, one player can throw the ball harder or throw it further away from the other player.

Perform no less than 10 catches, 5 with each hand.

Quick Catches:

The quick catches drill will force players to quickly get their hands into position. This drill requires two players to perform. To perform the drill, start anywhere on the court with your hands behind your back and your knees slightly bent. The other player will stand about 5 to 10 feet away with the basketball. The player with the ball will pass it to you. You must quickly get your hands in front of you and catch the ball before it hits you in the chest. To make the drill easier, the player with the ball can start further away and vice-versa to make things more difficult.

Perform no less than 10 passes.

Ball-Handling Drills

Toss the Ball Side to Side:

This drill improves hand eye coordination and develops a feel for the basketball. To perform the drill, stand upright with the basketball in one of your hands. With your arms in front of you, toss the ball to your opposite hand then and then back to the starting hand. Toss the basketball back and forth between each hand for the duration of the drill. Make sure to look straight and not on the ball. Also, be sure that only your fingertips are making contact with the ball. Try to perform the drill as quickly as possible. You can make the drill more difficult by starting with your arms shoulder width apart and slowly moving them outward. However, don't move your arms so far apart that you're unable to perform the drill.

Perform this drill for no less than 1 minute.

Ball Rotations Around Head:

Ball rotations can improve hand eye coordination and help players develop a feel for the ball. To perform the drill, stand upright with the basketball in one of your hands. Move the basketball around your head clockwise in a circular motion to your other hand. When the ball is in your opposite hand, continue to move it around your head to the starting hand. Continue to rotate the basketball around your head for the duration of the drill. You can increase the speed of the rotations to make the drill more difficult. You can change up the drill by reversing the direction of the rotations.

Perform this drill for no less than 1 minute.

Ball Rotations Around Waist:

To perform the drill, stand straight up with the basketball in one of your hands. Bring the ball to waist level and move it around the front of your body (clockwise) to your opposite hand. Continue rotating the ball around your body until it reaches the starting hand. The basketball should stay at waist level for the duration of the drill. Increase the speed of the rotations as time goes on and slow down if it is too difficult. Reverse the direction of the rotations to change up the drill.

Perform this drill for no less than 1 minute.

Ball Rotations Around Ankles:

Like the other rotation drills, this drill involves rotating the basketball in a circular motion around a part of your body. To perform the drill, squat down with your feet together and hold the basketball near your ankles. Rotate the basketball around your ankles in a clockwise motion. The ball should be passed to the opposite hand and end up in the starting hand to complete one rotation. You can increase the speed of the rotations to make things more difficult. Reverse the direction of the rotations around your ankles to change up the drill.

Perform this drill for no less than 1 minute.

Ball Rotation Combination:

The ball rotation combination drill combines all of the previous rotation drills together into one. The rotations will be performed one after another, and then you will start again from the first rotation. To perform the drill, stand straight up with the basketball in one of your hands and your arms at your sides. Bring the ball up to eye level and perform one ball rotation around your head. Then, perform one ball rotation around your waist. Lastly, bend down and perform one ball rotation around your ankles. Get back into the position and repeat all three rotations. You will continue to perform the three rotations for the duration of the drill. As with the individual rotations, you can increase the speed of your ball rotations as the drill progresses.

Perform this drill for no less than 1 minute.

Seated Bounces:

Seated bounces are to be performed while sitting. They can be performed where there isn't enough room to perform standing drills. To perform the drill, sit down on a chair, bench, or any elevated surface so that you are in a seated position with the ball. Use either hand to bounce the ball behind your feet to the opposite hand then back to the starting hand. The motion is similar to the crossover move just in a seated position. The drill is a great way to work on ball-handling skills while you are sitting down relaxing.

Perform this drill for any amount of time.

Seated Bounces (Variation):

This drill is a variation on the normal seated bounces drill. To perform the drill, sit down on any elevated surface with the basketball. With either hand bounce the ball behind your feet. When the ball is in the opposite hand, move the opposite foot back slightly. Now bounce the ball in front of that leg to the starting hand. When the ball is back in the starting hand, move your foot back to its original position and repeat. The drill should be performed quickly and your foot should move as quickly as you perform the move.

Perform this drill for any amount of time.

Fingertip Bounces:

Bouncing the ball with the fingertips will increase finger strength and improve a player's ability to control the basketball. To perform this drill, sit upright on the ground with the basketball. With either hand, bounce the ball with just your index finger. After performing a few bounces, move the ball to your middle finger. Continue bouncing the ball and switching fingers until all the digits of your hand have been used. Then, move the ball to your opposite hand and repeat the drill.

Perform this drill for any amount of time.

Figure Eight:

The figure eight is a ball-handling drill in which a player uses a series of quick bounces to navigate the ball around his/her legs in a figure eight motion. The bounces should be quick and only a few inches off the ground. To perform the drill, start with the ball and get into a low stance. Start dribbling the ball next to one of your feet. Bounce the ball around the outside of your leg and between your legs. Then, hand the ball off to the opposite hand and repeat with using the other leg. The ball should travel around both legs in a figure eight motion. You should only need to use your fingers to bounce the ball through your legs. Stay low and keep your eyes straight ahead for the duration of the drill.

Perform this drill for no less than 30 seconds.

Reverse Figure Eight:

The reverse figure eight is the same drill as the normal figure eight. The only difference is that the figure eight will be performed in the opposite direction. To perform this version, dribble the ball behind your back and through your legs. Pass the ball off to your opposite hand and bounce it around your opposite leg. Then, dribble it between your legs again.

Perform this drill for no less than 30 seconds.

Stationary crossover:

The stationary crossover drill is used to improve a player's ability to perform the crossover move. To perform this drill, start anywhere on the court with the ball. Stand with your legs shoulder with apart and get into a low stance. Perform the crossover move in front of your body. As soon as the ball reaches your opposite hand, perform another crossover. Continue to perform crossovers in this manner for the duration of the drill. The move should be performed quickly and the ball shouldn't bounce higher than knee level. Make sure to look straight ahead and don't look down while performing the drill. If you make a mistake during the drill or lose the ball, stop the time and resume when possible.

Perform this drill for no less than 30 seconds.

Stationary Behind-the-Back:

The stationary behind-the-back drill will improve a player's ability to perform the behind-the-back move. To perform the drill, start anywhere on the court with the ball. Stand with your feet shoulder width apart and get into a squatting position by bending your knees. Bounce the ball behind your back. The ball should be bounced from one hand to the other behind your back. As soon as the ball reaches the opposite hand, bounce it back to the other hand. Be sure to stay low and look straight ahead for the duration of the drill.

Perform this drill for no less than 30 seconds.

Stationary Between-the-Legs:

The stationary between the legs drill will improve a player's ability to perform the between-the-legs move. To perform the drill, start anywhere on the court with the ball. Stand with your feet shoulder width apart and get into a low stance. Dribble the ball between your legs in either direction. Catch the ball with your opposite hand, bring it in front of your body, and bounce it between your legs with the opposite hand. The movement of the ball will resemble the figure eight dribble except the ball will only be bounced between the legs.

Perform this drill for no less than 30 seconds.

Between-the-Legs Full Court:

To perform this drill, start on the baseline with the ball. Take a step forward while simultaneously bouncing the ball between your legs. Take a step with the opposite leg and bounce the ball between your legs again, this time from the opposite direction. Continue bouncing the ball between your legs for the entire length of the court. When you reach the opposite baseline, turn around and repeat the drill until you reach the starting position.

Perform this drill no less than 2 times.

Reverse Between-the-Legs Full Court:

The reverse between the legs full court drill is very similar to the normal version. The difference is that you will walk backward toward the opposite baseline. When you reach the opposite baseline, turn around and repeat the drill until you reach the starting position. Alternatively, you can perform the normal full court between-the-legs move to the opposite baseline then perform the reverse version back to the starting position.

Perform this drill no less than 2 times.

Crossover Full Court:

To perform the drill, start on the baseline with the ball. Perform the crossover move while simultaneously taking a step forward. The ball should move toward the foot you are stepping with. Be sure to look straight ahead and stay low while performing the crossover move. Continue to perform the crossover and step forward until you reach the opposite baseline. Then, turn around and continue the drill until you reach the starting position.

Perform the drill no less than 2 times.

Behind-the-Back Full Court:

To perform this drill, start on the baseline with the ball. Take a step forward and simultaneously bounce the ball behind your back. The ball should be bounced toward the foot you're stepping with. Continue performing the behind-the-back move and stepping forward until you reach the opposite baseline. Turn around and continue the drill until you reach the starting position. Stay low and look straight ahead for the duration of the drill. The move should be performed fluidly with each step.

Perform the drill no less than 2 times.

Two Basketballs:

You will need two basketballs for each of the subsequent ball-handling drills. Using two basketballs at the same time will allow players to develop ball-handling skills for both hands simultaneously. You can greatly increase your ball-handling skills by using two basketballs. However, the drills will be more difficult because you must focus your attention on both hands at the same time.

Simultaneous Dribble (Stationary):

To perform the drill, start anywhere on the court with a basketball in each hand. Squat down like you're getting into a triple threat stance. Start dribbling both simultaneously. Try to keep both basketballs in sync with each other. Start slowly at first, but gradually increase your dribbling speed each time you perform the drill. Stay low and try not to bounce the basketballs too high.

Perform this drill for no less than 30 seconds.

Simultaneous Dribble (Full Court):

To perform this drill, start at the baseline with a basketball in each hand. Stand with your feet shoulder width apart and get low. Dribble both basketballs simultaneously while slowly walking forward. Continue walking until you reach the opposite baseline. Then, turn around and return to the starting position. You can increase the difficulty of the drill by walking faster, jogging, or running. Stay in a low stance and keep the ball low to the ground for the duration of the drill.

Perform this drill no less than 2 times.

Alternating Dribble (Stationary):

To perform this drill, get into a stance with the basketballs. With a basketball in each hand, begin to dribble them. Alternate the bounces and try to maintain a rhythm. Also, try not to bounce the basketballs too high. Increase the speed of your bounces to make the drill more difficult.

Perform this drill for no less than 30 seconds.

Alternating Dribble (Full Court):

To perform this drill, stand at the baseline and get into a stance. With a basketball in each hand, begin to bounce them while walking forward. Alternate your dribbles while keeping the ball low to the ground. Be sure to stay in a low stance for the duration of the drill. Walk to the opposite baseline then return to the starting point. You can make the drill more difficult by increasing your walking speed, jogging, or running.

Perform this drill no less than 2 times.

One Low, One High:

To perform this drill, start by squatting down as if you're getting into a triple threat stance. With a basketball in each hand, begin to dribble them both simultaneously. Begin to lower the dribble height of one basketball and raise the height of the other. Maintain these heights for at least 10 seconds, and then switch the height of the two basketballs.

Perform this drill for no less than 45 seconds.

Circle Simultaneous Dribble:

To perform the drill, stand with your feet shoulder width apart and get low. With a basketball in both hands, begin to dribble both simultaneously. As soon as you start dribbling, begin to move both basketballs counterclockwise in a circular motion in front of your body. Your hands should guide each basketball until they reach the opposite hand. Continue dribbling in this manner for the duration of the drill. This drill can be performed in either a clockwise or counterclockwise motion.

Perform this drill for no less than 30 seconds.

Two Basketball Crossover:

To perform this drill, start by getting into a low stance. With a basketball in each hand, dribble both of them one time, simultaneously. Then, simultaneously perform a crossover with each basketball. As soon as each basketball reaches the opposite hand, perform one dribble and crossover again. Keep dribbling in this manner for the duration of the drill.

Perform this drill for no less than 30 seconds.

Defensive Drills

Defensive Slides:

The defensive slides drill is great for increasing lateral quickness. Lateral quickness is key component to playing solid defense. To perform the drill, begin at the corner of the baseline in a defensive stance. Perform a defensive slide to the free throw line, the half court line, the opposite free throw line, and finally, the opposite baseline corner. When you reach the opposite baseline corner, start again and touch all four spots in reverse. Don't forget to stay low and keep your arms out. You can add a time limit to make the drill more challenging.

Perform this drill no less than 3 times.

You can also add a ball-handler to the drill to make it more of a simulation. Defend the ball-handler down the court by sliding in a defensive stance. The ball-handler will zigzag and change speeds constantly to make the drill more difficult.

Perform this drill no less than 2 times.

Close Out Drill:

The close out drill can improve the speed and technique of a player's close out. To perform the drill, stand at the baseline with the ball. Another player will stand at the free throw or three-point line. Pass the ball to the other player and sprint forward. When you are one to two steps away from the other person, close out as quickly as possible. Remember to use choppy steps before reaching the person with the ball. Also, remember to put your hands up when closing out to defend a shot attempt. If you do not have a partner, perform a close out to a random location on the court.

Perform no less than 10 close outs.

Quick Feet:

The quick feet drill helps to improve a player's foot speed. To perform this drill, get into a defensive stance and move your feet up and down as quickly as possible. The motion of body should resemble running in place. The difference is that this drill is performed while in a defensive stance. Keep your feet moving for the duration of the drill. Don't forget to stay low and on the balls of your feet.

Perform the drill for no less than 30 seconds.

Rebounding Drills

Backboard Taps:

The backboard tap drill can improve a player's rebounding ability. It can help players develop a habit of keeping the ball high while rebounding. To perform the drill, stand in front of the backboard with the ball. Jump and tap the ball against the backboard without letting go of it. Do not let go of the ball after you have tapped the backboard. As soon as your feet touch the ground, jump again and perform another tap. After the final backboard tap, perform a layup to finish the drill. Remember to keep the ball up high for the duration of the drill.

Perform no less than 10 backboard taps.

Backboard Put-Back Drill:

The backboard put back drill shares some similarities to the previous rebounding drill. The difference is that players won't bring the ball down with them. This drill will develop rebounding ability and timing. To perform the drill, throw the ball off the backboard and let it bounce back to you. Jump and catch the ball in mid-air after it bounces off the backboard. As soon as you catch the ball, toss it off the backboard again. This will count as one put-back. As soon as your feet touch the ground, jump to perform another put-back. Keep performing put backs for the duration of the drill. Remember to keep your hands up for the entire of the drill.

Perform no less than 10 put backs.

Swim Move Drill:

The swim move is used to get the inside position when attempting to rebound. The swim move drill improves the ability to perform the swim move technique against a defender. The drill requires at least two players. To perform the drill, stand anywhere on the court with the other player standing directly in front of you. Perform the swim move to get in front of this player. As soon as you get in front, stop and box out the other player. Next, it will be the other player's turn to perform the swim move on you. You both will alternate for the duration of the drill.

Perform the swim move drill for no less than 1 minute.

2-Man Backboard Rebounds:

This drill allows players to improve their rebounding and timing. The drill requires two players and each player must start on a block. Each player will bounce the ball off the backboard to the other player. Both players must keep their hands up and be ready to catch the ball as it bounces toward them to successfully perform the drill. To perform this drill, each player will start on one of the blocks on opposite sides of the paint. Start with the basketball and toss it off the backboard to the other player. The ball should hit the backboard above the rim and bounce toward that player. The other player will jump to catch the ball and toss it back off the backboard while still in the air. Both players will continue bouncing the ball off the backboard to each other for the duration of the drill.

Perform this drill for at least 1 minute or 20 bounces.

Chapter 15 | Terminology

Air ball - a field goal attempt that fails to make contact with the rim or backboard.

Alley-oop – a play in which one player passes to a teammate (that is already in the air) for a finish at the rim.

And 1 – describes a situation in which a player is fouled while shooting, scores the field goal, and gets a free throw attempt.

Assist – a play in which one player passes the ball to a teammate who then immediately scores.

Assistant coach – a coach who assists the head coach in making decisions concerning the team.

Backboard – the square shaped board attached to the rim.

Backcourt – the guard positions on the floor.

Backcourt violation – occurs when the offensive team fails to bring the ball across half-court within a certain amount of time.

Backdoor – a cut that is made behind a defender and is angled toward the basket.

Back screen – a screen set by an offensive player for a teammate who then cuts to the goal.

Ball fake – a fake pass to a teammate.

Ball hog – a player that doesn't like to pass the ball and attempts to score whenever he/she receives the ball on offense.

Ball reversal – when the ball is passed from one side of the court to the other, usually around the perimeter.

Ball-side – the side of the court where the ball is located.

Baseline – the lines located at the both ends of the court. These lines run the width of the court.

Behind-the-back pass – a skilled pass made to a teammate behind the back that requires a certain amount of skill and accuracy.

Benchwarmer – a player that gets little to no playing time.

Block – when a defender deflects an offensive player's field goal attempt.

Block (lane) – the rectangular box located on the both sides of the lane.

Blocking foul – occurs when a defensive player is not set when attempting a charge.

Blowout – occurs when a team wins a basketball game by a large margin.

Bounce pass – a pass that is bounced off the court to a teammate.

Box out – when a player uses his/her body to stop an opposing player from securing a rebound.

Breakaway – when a player gains possession of the ball, usually as a result of a turnover, and breaks away from the defense.

Brick – a missed field goal that bounces off the rim.

Buzzer beater – a field goal that is attempted just before time runs out.

Center – a low post position that is primarily responsible for rebounding and defending the paint.

Charge – when an offensive player collides with a defender that is set (standing still).

Chest pass – a pass made from the chest.

Clutch – a player that performs well in the later stages of the game while under pressure.

Coach – the person that directs, instructs, and trains a team. A coach makes decisions regarding how a team will play during a game.

Crossover dribble – an offensive move in which a player moves the ball from one hand to the other by bouncing it in front of his/her body.

Cut – when an offensive player runs toward the goal expecting to receive a pass and score.

Dead ball – when gameplay is halted as a result of the ball being out of bounds or foul.

Defense – the actions of a team while defending their goal against the opposing team.

Defensive foul – a foul committed while playing defense. Ex. Reaching foul, blocking foul, shooting foul.

Defensive rebound – a rebound secured by a player defensive player.

Deny – to place a hand in the trajectory of a pass to keep an offensive player from receiving the ball.

Drop Step – a wide powerful step toward the goal. The move is usually made from the block by a post player.

Double-Double – occurs when a player records double figures in two separate categories. Ex. Shooting, rebounding, etc.

Double dribbling violation – occurs when a player resumes dribbling after stopping.

Double team – when two players defend the ball-handler simultaneously.

Drive – when the ball-handler dribbles toward the goal in a half court setting.

Dunk – when a player forcibly throws the ball through the rim.

Elbow – the top corner of the free throw line.

Euro Step – an offensive move in which the ball-handler takes two steps in separate directions to avoid defenders.

Fadeaway – a special jump shot in which the shooter leans back while shooting.

Fast break – when the offensive team quickly brings the ball up the court and outnumbers the defense.

Field goal – an attempted shot at the goal.

Finger roll – a layup in which the shooter rolls the ball off his/her fingers.

First step – describes the quickness of the first step taken when driving to the basket.

Flagrant foul – a foul involving excessive or violent contact.

Floater – a field goal with a high, soft arc that is typically shot with one hand.

Foul – illegal contact made by a player.

Free throw – an uncontested shot that is awarded to a player that is fouled.

Free throw line - the line at the top of the lane.

Free throw line extended – an imaginary extension of the free throw line that runs the width of the court.

Front court – the forward and center positions on the floor.

Full court – describes the entire length of the court.

Full court press – a press defense that spans the length of the court.

Goaltending – when a player interferes with a field goal that is touching the rim or on its way down toward the rim.

Guard – a player that plays on the perimeter when his/her team is on offense.

Half court – half the length of the court.

Half court defense – a defense that takes place on one half of the court.

Half court offense – an offense that takes place on one half of the court.

High post – the top of the lane.

Hook shot – a field goal shot in a sweeping motion over the top of the body with the outside hand. The shooter is usually positioned perpendicular to the goal when attempting this shot.

Inbound pass – a pass made from out of bounds after a timeout, dead ball, made field goal, or change in possession.

Jump ball – occurs when two opposing players have their hands on the ball, but neither has possession.

Jump shot – A shot that is released while the shooter is in the air.

Lane – the painted area that runs from the baseline to the free throw line.

Layup – a field goal attempt in which shooter jumps into the air and shoots the ball at close range, usually off the backboard.

Loose ball – occurs when the ball is in play but no team has possession of it.

Long range – area behind the 3-point line.

Low post – the area around the basket, but outside of the paint.

Man to man defense – a defensive strategy in which each defender guards one offensive player.

Mid-range – area inside of the 3-point line, but outside of the lane.

Motion offense – an offensive strategy used to neutralize a defensive height advantage or utilize offensive quickness.

Offense – the actions of an offensive team while attempting to score the ball.

Offensive foul – a foul committed by an offensive player.

Offensive Rebound – a rebound secured by an offensive player.

One and one – a situation in which an offensive player shoots one free throw and is awarded a second if the first shot is made. Occurs after a non-shooting foul while the opposing team is in the bonus.

Open man – an offensive player that is unguarded.

Out of bounds – the area of the court outside of the boundary lines.

Outlet pass – a pass made directly after a defensive rebound to begin a fast break.

Over and back violation – occurs when an offensive player crosses back over the half court line and touches the ball without a defender touching it first.

Over the back foul – occurs when a player attempts to secure a rebound and makes contact with an opposing player without having the inside position.

Overhead pass – a pass released while the ball is over the ball-handler's head.

Overtime – any additional gameplay after the end of regulation. Occurs when the score is tied at the end of the game.

Paint – see key.

Palming – when a player holds the ball in one hand using his/her fingers.

Pass – when the basketball is intentionally thrown to a teammate.

Passer – the offensive player that passes the ball.

Passing lane – the trajectory of a potential pass.

Penalty – occurs when one team commits a specific number of fouls. After this number has been reached, any additional fouls will result in the opposing team shooting one to two free throws.

Penetration – occurs when an offensive player dribbles or passes the ball toward the goal.

Perimeter – see Mid-range.

Pick and pop – an offensive strategy in which an offensive player sets a screen then moves away from the basket.

Pick and roll – an offensive strategy in which an offensive player sets a screen then rolls toward the basket.

Pin down – when a player sets a screen, turns, and posts up in the low post.

Pivot – to turn on one foot while in possession of the ball.

Pivot foot – the foot that must remain on the ground and stationary while a player is in possession of the ball.

Point guard – the guard that usually brings the ball up the court and sets up the offense.

Possession – to have control of the ball.

Possession arrow – establishes which team will gain possession of the ball after a jump ball situation.

Post – see Low post.

Post man – the player that posts up during the game.

Post up – occurs when a player uses his/her body to block off the defender in the post on offense.

Power dribble – a powerful two-handed dribble used near the basket.

Power forward – a flexible post position that is usually responsible for rebounding and defending the paint.

Press – a defensive strategy that increases the level of defensive pressure placed on the offense.

Put back – when an offensive player tips, dunks, shoots a missed field goal.

Quarter – competitive basketball games are broken up into fourths or quarters for professional and amateur play, excluding collegiate basketball.

Range – describes the distance at which an offensive player is able to score the basketball.

Reaching foul – occurs when illegal contact made by a defender while attempting to steal the ball.

Run – when one team scores several consecutive points outscoring the opposing team. Ex. the team is on a 19-2 run.

Run and gun – an offensive strategy in which players try to quickly move the ball up the court and take a quick shot.

Set shot – a field goal attempt in which the shooter does not jump into the air.

Scoreboard – the board that displays the scores for the two teams, the amount of time remaining in the quarter or half, which team has possession of the ball, and how many fouls each team has accumulated.

Screen – when an offensive player uses his/her body to block a defender's path.

Scrimmage – a practice game that simulates a real game.

Shoot around – a shooting oriented practice used to prepare for a game.

Shooter – the player that is attempting a field goal. Describes a player adept at shooting.

Shooting guard – the guard position responsible for shooting and scoring the ball.

Short-range – the area of the court directly around the goal.

Shot clock – displays the remaining time allowed for an offensive possession.

Sideline – the lines that run the length of the court.

Sixth man – the first player subbed into the game.

Small forward – A versatile position capable of various styles of play. This position is usually responsible for defending and scoring.

Square up – to turn your body so that it faces the goal.

Steal – occurs when a defender gains possession of the ball by intercepting a pass or taking the ball from an offensive player.

Strong side – see ball side.

Substitute – a player on the bench that replaces a player in the game.

Team fouls – the total fouls accumulated by a team.

Technical foul – a special type of foul called when a player or coach displays some type of unsportsmanlike conduct.

Timeout – a short break in gameplay.

Tip in – when a player scores the ball by tipping a missed field back into the rim.

Touch – describes a shooter's ability shoot the ball lightly off the rim.

Three-point field goal – a field goal attempted behind the 3-point line.

Three-point play – a play in which the ball-handler is fouled in the act of shooting, scores the basket, and makes the subsequent free throw. The three-point play is also known as an old fashioned three pointer because the three point line was not introduced until 1980.

Three-second violation – a violation in which an offensive player is inside the painted area for three seconds. The ball will be awarded to the opposing team.

Transition defense – the process of switching from offense to defense immediately after an offensive possession.

Transition offense – the process of switching from defense to offense immediately after playing defense.

Trap - when two defenders attempt to block an offensive player's path and make that player unable to progress further.

Traveling violation – occurs when a player moves both feet while in possession of the ball without first taking a dribble.

Triple double – occurs when a player records double figures in three separate statistical categories. Ex. 10 points, 10 rebounds, 10 assists.

Triple threat position – an offensive position that prepares a player to shoot, pass, or dribble.

Turnover – occurs when an offensive player makes a mistake that results in the opposing team gaining possession of the ball. This could be the result of a steal, an offensive foul, the ball-handler stepping out of bounds, or the ball-handler throwing the ball out of bounds.

Uncontested shot – an undefended field goal attempt.

Weak side – the side of the court, from the center of the paint to the sideline, which is opposite the ball.

Wing – the wing is the free throw line extended behind the 3-point line. Can also describe the small forward or 3 position.

Zone defense – a defensive strategy in which each player on defense defends a specific area of the court.

Zone offense - an offensive strategy used to counteract a zone defense.

Made in the USA
San Bernardino, CA
26 June 2014